W9-BBX-824

"*The Woman's Belly Book* is for every woman who has ever stood in front of her mirror, sucking in her belly, wishing to be different. Lisa teaches us how to cherish the power center within us with a wealth of exercises, modern science, and wisdom from ancient cultures."
—LAVINIA PLONKA, author of *What Are You Afraid Of? A body/mind guide to courageous living*

"*The Woman's Belly Book* is a soulful antidote to the cultural indoctrination into body hatred experienced by contemporary women of all ages. Brainwashed to control, sculpt, and distrust our bodies, we desperately need new insights and tools to begin to appreciate, honor, and nourish our core essence and physical being. Many other books inspire us to 'talk the talk' of making peace with our bodies, but *The Woman's Belly Book* shows us how to 'walk the walk.'"
—MARGO MAINE, PhD, author of *The Body Myth: The pressure on women to be perfect*

"*The Woman's Belly Book* blends yoga, myth, playfulness, and practicality as it invites women to honor the belly as a source of vitality and creativity. This book is a rich resource for women recovering from eating disorders, especially as they dare to open themselves to a fuller relationship to their body and their womanhood."
—SHEILA M. REINDL, EdD, author of *Sensing the Self: Women's recovery from bulimia*

"This charming, insightful, and informative book encourages women to embrace the center of their bodies and celebrate the wisdom of their feminine nature. Truly a treasure!"
—ANITA JOHNSTON, PhD, author of *Eating in the Light of the Moon: How women can transform their relationship with food through myths, metaphors and storytelling*

"This book is utterly life changing. It touches on something very personal and powerful for all women. *The Woman's Belly Book* is one of the most influential books I've ever read."
—KAYLEIGH

continued on back pages

The Woman's Belly Book

•

Finding Your Treasure Within

Lisa Sarasohn

The Woman's Belly Book:
Finding Your Treasure Within
by Lisa Sarasohn

Copyright © 2003 by Self-Health Education, Inc.
Illustrations, text, and book design by Lisa Sarasohn
Author photograph by Totsie Marine
Poem by Carol Barre used by permission

Self-Health Education, Inc.
PO Box 1783
Asheville, NC 28802-1783
http://www.loveyourbelly.com

NOTE TO THE READER: Consult with your health care provider in advance to determine the suitability of the exercises and activities described in this book for you. The information provided here is for educational purposes only. It is not intended for the diagnosis or treatment of any physical or emotional disorder.

Additional copies may be ordered from the publisher online at http://www.loveyourbelly.com. Quantity discounts for organizations supporting women's well-being are available.

ISBN 0-9745481-1-1

Printed in the United States of America

This book is dedicated
to you.

Contents

Acknowledgements

What amounts to a small nation of women and men has helped me to bring this book into being. I thank each and every one of you. You've inspired, challenged, instructed, aided, cheered, and encouraged me for years. You know who you are.

My thanks go to all the women who have sponsored my workshops. Together, we've created the opportunity for so many women to become belly-proud.

Each woman who has participated in my workshops and responded to my writing has been a shining source of inspiration. As we've shared our stories we've become belly buddies, belly friends. Thank you.

I'm grateful to my family for their enduring support.

The Unitarian Universalist Women's Federation kindly assisted me in producing the related instructional video. Thank you.

I honor all the women who have held the red thread of women's wisdom through each generation, passing it on to the next.

And I thank the Muse in all her many guises.

The Woman's Belly Book

· · ·

WELCOME

At this moment, I imagine you're wondering: Is this book for me? Will it make a difference in my life?

Here's what I can tell you:

This book is about valuing your body and yourself.

It's about knowing your body's center—your belly—as the site of your soul-power, wellspring of your physical, emotional, and spiritual vitality.

My message is this: The life energy focused in your belly is the source of your passion and creativity. Your courage and confidence. Your capacity to love fully. Your intuition, insight, and sense of purpose. It is your release from stress, your guide to good health. It is the origin of your inner strength.

What I'm saying is: You can develop the source energy concentrated in your body's center. You can direct its expression to enhance every dimension of your life.

This book is a guide for doing exactly that.

But still, is this book for you? It's for you if:

- you've dieted to "trim your tummy." Now you want to get a better take on what your belly is all about.

- you've had enough of feeling bad about your body. You realize your belly will never be board-flat. You're ready to feel good about yourself as a whole.

- you suspect that if you could make peace with your belly, you could tap into a wealth of creativity, wisdom, and inner guidance.

- you want to take charge of your sexual energy and fully own your pro-creative power.

- you've had a hysterectomy or given birth by C-section and still feel torn up. You want to feel whole again.

- you're passing through menopause and want to access the core energy that's becoming all the more available to you at this stage of your life.

- you already enjoy yoga, Tai Chi, martial arts, African dance, or Middle Eastern dance and you want to experience another approach to body-centered movement.

- you're looking for an invigorating, power-centering exercise program you can easily do in five minutes.

- you're seeking a body-centered path to personal and spiritual empowerment.

This book *may* be for you—in conjunction with appropriate medical or psychotherapeutic attention—if you've struggled with an eating disorder, experienced abdominal pain or illness, or survived assault focused on your belly. Please consult with your health care provider to determine whether and how this book can be of service to you.

This book is for you and your daughter, for you and your mother, as a foundation for sharing the experience of your womanhood and fostering respect across the generations.

This book is for you and your friends as a basis for supporting each other in finding your own ways to value your belly, your body, yourself.

In these times, it takes guts—courage, determination, and daring—to consider honoring your belly and the soul-power it contains. And so I welcome you, a gutsy woman, to *The Woman's Belly Book.*

Lisa Sarasohn
Asheville, NC
September 9, 2003

• • •

Dear Belly

Dear belly, please
    forgive me
    for:
          girdles
          corsets
          attempts to be twig–thin

          nourishment not taken
          food crammed in

          words unsaid
          cries stifled
          rage unspoken
          rage unscreamed

          joy denied
          desire denied
          power denied

          constriction
          restriction
          prescription
          proscription
             collusion with this culture's
             breeding for non–being

I embrace you, belly.
Life fire, I salute you.

          I release you
          to live me, breathe me
          in your own full rhythm.

• • •

Finding Treasure

Suppose you found an earthen bowl wrapped in a tattered cloth and bound with metal bands.

You remove the straps and take away the cloth. There's nothing very special about the bowl. It's not stylish. It's not fashionable.

Some people say your bowl is shameful. Voices all around you tell you to lose it, hide it.

For a time, you might believe those voices. You might spend many years and much effort trying to lose or hide your bowl. But no matter what you do, it stays with you.

One day, for whatever reason, you take another look at the bowl. It has a lid, and the lid is stuck on tight. You can't see what's within. But when you shake the bowl, you hear something rattling inside.

Whether you know it or not, there's treasure inside this bowl, seven jewels that can:

- keep you looking and feeling great
- spice up your sexual pleasure
- magnify your courage and confidence
- fill your heart to overflowing
- unleash your creativity
- enhance your intuition
- make your dreams come true.

There's one more gem inside the bowl, a constant source of light that gives all the other jewels their sparkle.

You and only you can open this bowl.

But how? To lift the lid and claim your treasure all you need to do is...love the bowl.

Deepening Your Search

●

What is this earthen bowl of treasure that you've found? It's your belly. And loving your belly enables you to claim the treasure inside.

What are you going to do? If you're like most women, you've always been told that your body isn't good enough, that your belly is shameful. As far as you may know, there's nothing good at all about a woman's belly unless it's flat and hard. You may have spent many years and much effort trying to lose your belly, trying to hide it from sight.

I know that the idea of loving your belly might be challenging. Okay, it might be rather unconventional. Well, given the culture's bias against women's bellies, loving your belly might actually require some courage.

But tell me: Whose body is it, anyway? Who has the say-so? Who benefits when you belittle your belly? Who benefits when you befriend your belly and give yourself room to breathe? It's your body, your belly, your life. Whose permission do you need to love yourself?

I know that loving your belly is a strange and wild idea. But what's the alternative? Do you really want to miss out on the treasure that's so close to home?

●

Here's the plan—

The first step is unwrapping the bowl. You'll learn to let your belly breathe. And I'll help you cancel the common misconceptions that give woman's belly a bad name. You'll discover how your belly boosts your physical health and emotional well-being. Learning the truth will change the way you think about your belly.

The next step is lifting the lid and opening the bowl, creating a loving relationship with your belly. You already know how to love. I'll suggest fifteen playful ways you can extend your affection to your body's core, centralizing your self-esteem.

Loving your belly enables you to open the bowl and claim the treasure waiting inside. For each of the seven jewels you'll find, I'll suggest patterns of breathing, imaging, and moving. These belly-energizing exercises will make the jewels shine all the more brightly for you.

● ● ●

The tips for loving your belly and the belly-energizing exercises you'll find here are similar to those I've shared with hundreds of women in my weekly classes, workshops, and weekend retreats. They're the fruit of my more than twenty years as a yoga teacher, yoga therapist, bodyworker, and health educator.

I initially developed this material for my own healing. These inquiries and exercises enabled me to make peace with my belly and move beyond my own eating disorder. I'll tell you my story later. For now, know that you're joining an expanding circle of women who share this adventure with you.

Throughout these pages you'll find women's words about their own experience becoming belly-proud. Consider these voices to be your personal chorus of support.

As we begin, please note that I'm not asking you to engage in a self-improvement program. I am inviting you to find out what the earthen bowl you've discovered, your belly, is really worth.

Sure, you may want to change some of the ways you think, feel, breathe, value, choose, move. I encourage you to make such changes only because you're being true to an ever-deepening sense of who you already are.

Why bother loving your belly? Because that's the only way you can claim the treasure that's waiting inside.

Still, you might be wondering: Will loving my belly flush away the fat? Will it trim my tummy?

If you are asking those questions, there's another one to consider: What is your underlying concern?

Perhaps you hope that trimming your tummy will allow you to like yourself better. (I've been there! And if this is your concern, you're in company with many other women.)

In otherwise healthy women, I suspect that extra belly fat can function as protective padding, a shield from self-criticism and a buffer against the feeling of shame. It's an intriguing possibility: Will replacing self-criticism with self-respect allow that extra layer of fat to melt away?

• • •

Will loving my belly trim my tummy?

This question leads to another: What is your underlying concern?

Perhaps you're concerned that the size of your belly might be a symptom of serious illness.

> Abdominal bloating, swelling, or distension can be a sign of conditions ranging from food intolerance to uterine fibroids and several kinds of cancer. To eliminate the possibility of a physical ailment, consult with your health care provider— especially if you're experiencing abdominal pain.

Perhaps you're concerned about the health risks that might be associated with extra fat around your body's midsection.

> If you are at risk for conditions such as diabetes, heart disease, cancer, or stroke, consult with your health care provider to create a plan for minimizing your risk.

If that's an experiment you'd like to make, I'm glad to help you do so. Check out the inquiries in *Lifting the Lid*, particularly *Bless Yourself* (p. 33) and *Shield Yourself in Style* (p. 45).

Does loving your belly dissolve excess fat? Does energizing your belly with movement and breath strengthen your abs? That's been my experience. Tell me about yours.

As you love your belly, "trimming the tummy" may become less of a concern. In fact, the problem itself may disappear as you turn your attention toward self-affirmation.

Again, I want to emphasize that I'm not making any judgments about belly size or shape. I'm not saying big bellies are better than small bellies. I'm not saying flat bellies are better than round bellies.

I am saying: Love your belly, lose the shame. Honor and exercise your belly as the source of your inner strength—that's the best way I know to claim your inner treasure.

Why bother loving your belly? There's one more reason.

Whatever happens to the center happens to the whole. As you learn to love your body's center, you're on the fast track to loving your whole self.

•

I rode the roller coaster of dieting and deprivation and starving and depression. I felt I was only worthy if I looked the way others wanted me to look. My life felt like I was swimming upstream.

Then I began looking inside and started to really glean the truth about myself, finally glimpsing my essence. I discovered that none of it had anything to do with the way I looked....

As I learned these lessons about my spirit, my internal Self, I began standing taller, smiling more, moving with more purpose, and walking the path of self-love and acceptance.

—Alison

• • •

• • •

Unwrapping the Gift

Discovering Your Inner Source

You've found an earthen bowl wrapped in a tattered cloth and bound tightly with metal bands. There's treasure inside. But how will you get to it?

Your first step is removing the metal bands. You'll give yourself room to breathe.

Then you'll take away the tattered cloth, revealing the bowl. Appreciating your belly, you'll discover your inner source.

Appreciating Your Belly
•

Your belly's potential role in dispelling depression may surprise you. Its role in moving life energy through your body may be new to you. And its role in providing a place for your organs of digestion, elimination, and reproduction may seem obvious.

Here you'll find a brief introduction to your belly as it contributes to your physical health, your emotional well-being, and the flow of vital energy through your body.

You'll also find practical ways your belly can help you to release stress, relax into restful sleep, and enjoy more vitality.

The information and skills you'll find here will help you to revalue your body's center. You may begin to suspect that your belly is your best friend for being healthy and happy in many dimensions of your life.

Appreciating your belly allows you to consider the possibility that it's home to your soul-power.

•

Honoring this very feminine center gives me a new sense of myself and my worth as a woman, my power. —Amy

Give yourself room to breathe

Loosen your belt, unzip your zipper, let out your waistband. Take off the tummy-crushing pantyhose, shed the tight skirt. Put on something that fits you comfortably around your waist and hips.

You can do it. As one woman says, "I don't want to wear anything that interferes with my breathing. Bring on the elastic waistbands!" You, too, deserve clothes that kindly give you room to breathe.

This is the pivotal point, and you'll see these words several times: Your physical health and your emotional well-being depend on your capacity to breathe deeply. And breathing deeply depends on letting your belly move out and in with each cycle of the breath.

When your clothes allow your belly to move with the breath, you can enjoy the benefits of breathing fully and deeply.

■

Here's how—

1• Loosen your belt or waistband. Sit with your palms resting lightly on your lower abdomen. That's all there is to it. Simply notice: What happens as you breathe?

2• You may not notice anything. That's fine. Or, you may feel your belly moving out and away from your spine with your incoming breath. You may sense it sinking back toward your spine with your outgoing breath.

Take a few moments to experience the rhythm of your breathing and how that rhythm plays out in the center of your body.

•

Refuse to wear uncomfortable pants, even if they make you look really thin. Promise me you'll never wear pants that bind or tug or hurt, pants that have an opinion about how much you've just eaten. The pants may be lying! —Annie Lamott

• • •

Cancel five misconceptions

As you recognize these misconceptions for what they are, you can choose for yourself how to value your body's center. You can make the choices that truly enhance your health and promote your well-being.

• Misconception #1:

Women of all ages can and should have a flat belly.

Nature does not intend a woman to look like a ten year-old boy. In fact, nature designs a woman's belly to shelter and nurture new life. A woman's belly holds and protects her womb, promoting the survival of the human species.

Nature expresses itself through genetics. Fewer than ten out of one hundred women have the genes for a fat-free midriff— when they're in their teens and twenties, that is.

• Misconception #2:

Big-bellied women have always been unfashionable.

Although fashion dictates flat bellies for women now, in other times round bellies have been in vogue. In 15th- through 17th-century Europe, for example, the bigger a woman's belly, the sexier she was considered to be. Women's clothes were styled to make the belly look grand.

Going back further in time, archeological evidence suggests that our ancestors celebrated the power of woman's belly to birth, nurture, and renew the world. Our ancestors considered woman's belly to be sacred, not shameful. Maybe our ancestors got it right.

• Misconception #3:

> *The best thing you can do for your belly is to make your abdominal muscles rock-hard. Failing that, hold your breath in and "suck it up" all day.*

Your physical health and emotional well-being depend on your capacity to breathe fully and deeply. When you make your abdominal muscles rigid, you restrict your breath. When you don't give yourself room to breathe, you're cutting yourself off from life.

• Misconception #4:

> *If you can't flatten your belly any other way, wear control-top pantyhose, tummy shapers, and tight pants—they're harmless.*

See above.

• Misconception #5:

> *A round belly on a woman means she's lazy, gluttonous, and slutty; her appetites are insatiable.*

Woman's belly is a symbol with great significance. It's a sign of woman's capacity to nourish herself, to feel and fulfill her desires. It's a robust visual reminder that woman's body contains an awesome power—the capacity to bring forth new life.

•

The belly is the zip code of the soul.
—Jeanette

• • •

Take a brief tour

Picture your belly as, well, a bowl. With your pelvis as its sturdy base, your belly envelops all your vital organs except for lungs, heart, and brain. Even these organs depend on your belly for their survival.

Organs

Your abdomen contains your organs of digestion and elimination—stomach, liver, gall bladder, pancreas, small intestine, kidneys, urinary bladder, large intestine. It contains your reproductive organs—ovaries, uterus, vagina. And it contains other tissues essential to your immunity, your nervous system, and the circulation of your blood.

Muscles

Your abdominal muscles help give your belly bowl its structure. Four layers of muscle, each with its fibers oriented in a different direction, contain and protect your vital organs. These muscles move your torso as well, enabling you to make a variety of twists and turns.

Moving in from the skin surface, the first two layers are muscle pairs: the external and internal obliques. They run diagonally on each side of your body from your ribs to the top ridges of your pelvis. Their fibers run at right angles to each other, creating an x-shaped pattern.

Next, the rectus abdominis runs vertically from your ribs and the base of your breastbone to your pubic bone. The transversus abdominis is the deepest layer of muscle. Its fibers run horizontally, creating a cross-shaped pattern with the fibers of the rectus above.

Strong abdominal muscles hold your vital organs securely in place. They support your spine, help prevent lower back pain, and make your posture graceful.

• • •

Diaphragm

Your belly bowl's lid is your diaphragm, the broad muscle at the base of your lungs. The diaphragm rests directly upon the organs packed into your abdomen below.

Your diaphragm draws breath into your lungs by moving downward. Each time your diaphragm descends it presses upon your abdominal organs. To inhale fully, your diaphragm must descend fully. When your abdominal muscles—and your clothing—allow your belly to expand, they permit your abdominal organs to move downward and outward, accommodating your diaphragm's descent.

Your abdominal muscles and the clothes you wear determine how freely your diaphragm can move and how fully you can breathe. If your abdomen is rigid it restricts your diaphragm and makes your breathing shallow, increasing your sense of stress.

When your abdominal muscles are toned but not tight, and your clothing allows your belly to move, your diaphragm is also free to move and deepen your breathing, increasing your sense of self-assurance.

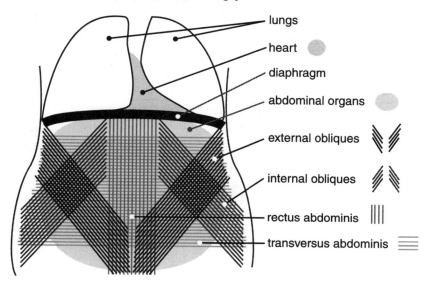

lungs

heart

diaphragm

abdominal organs

external obliques

internal obliques

rectus abdominis

transversus abdominis

A Sketch of Abdominal Anatomy

• • •

Be healthy

Your physical health and your emotional well-being depend on your capacity to breathe deeply, transforming air into life energy.

It's possible to cut your belly out of the loop, hold it tight and sniff at the air with just your nose, shoulders, and chest. But that's a sure recipe for building up tension and stress. Such shallow breathing reduces the supply of oxygen to your body and mind.

When you breathe deeply, letting your belly move out and in with each breath, you're giving your body and mind the generous supply of oxygen they need. Tension evaporates and instead you feel calm, energized, alert, relaxed.

Helping you to breathe deeply is only part of the story. Your belly also helps you to digest food, turning what you eat into fuel that powers your body and mind.

Remember a time when you went without food for a while—perhaps you missed a meal or two. How did you feel? Did you get tired and grumpy? How did you feel after you ate something nourishing? What made the difference?

Your belly, through its capacity for digestion, transformed food into life energy. We can take that for granted, but it's quite a miracle.

Not everything you eat is a nutrient. Food contains fiber and other matter that your body must eliminate. Elimination is not a pretty subject, but neither is constipation. Your belly does the important job of solid waste disposal.

Your belly also helps circulate blood and lymph through your body. As your belly moves out and in with your breath, it pumps these nourishing and cleansing fluids up from your lower body to your heart.

The organs and tissues within your belly strengthen your immunity to disease not only by circulating lymph but also by eliminating bacteria, removing toxins, and filtering your blood.

•

My husband is a paramedic. He works on an ambulance and brings home every virus imaginable. He gets sick. I don't. I do my belly exercises. —Teresa

• • •

CENTERING BREATH

Here it is—the deep abdominal breathing that enhances your physical health and promotes your emotional well-being. (If you have a serious medical condition, please review the *Practice Pointers* on p. 66.)

■

Here's how—

1• Give your belly room to breathe. Unhitch your waistband, loosen your belt, unzip your zipper. Sit or stand comfortably. Or lie on your back with a pillow under your knees to ease your lower back. Place your palms upon your lower abdomen.

2• Notice what's happening underneath your hands. You might sense a wave-like motion, your belly expanding away from your spine as you inhale and then sinking back toward your spine as you exhale.

3• If you don't see or sense any movement, that's okay. You can jump-start the process by actively pulling your belly in toward your spine as you exhale. Then release the contraction and allow your belly to relax. As it expands naturally—you don't need to push it outward—your belly draws the breath in, beginning the inhalation.

4• Continue, keeping your mouth closed and allowing the breath to move evenly in and out through your nose.

5• Feel the gentle rhythm, allowing your belly to expand and draw the breath in, then to sink back toward your spine and send the breath out.

6• Continue observing your belly and your breathing for ten or more cycles of breath. How do you feel?

Gradually return your attention to your whole body and to the present moment.

Sleep easy

Restful sleep is key to being healthy. Your belly can help ease you into dreamland. (If you're pregnant, see the *Practice Pointers* on p. 67.)

■

Here's how—

1• Lie on your back with your legs fully extended; place a pillow under your knees to ease your lower back.

2• Keeping your mouth closed, inhale slowly through your nose, expanding your belly to draw the breath in.

3• As you hold the breath in, contract your belly and pull it down toward your spine.

4• Holding the breath, tense the muscles in your legs, arms, face, chest, back, and buttocks—contracting every muscle from the outer edges of your body toward the center.

5• Now, still holding the breath in and keeping every muscle tight, push your belly out and hold it out for a slow count of five.

6• Open your mouth and exhale slowly. At the same time, totally relax all of your muscles.

Repeat as many as five times. You may notice how restlessness dissolves, giving way to repose.

Dispel depression

Your mood happens in your mind. But are mind and body really so distinct? Thoughts, feelings, and physical experience seem to overlap and interweave. The mind-belly connection is especially intimate.

Your belly is home to a major portion of the nervous system—the enteric nervous system, or ENS—that lines your entire gastrointestinal tract. Your "gut brain" communicates with your brain up top through the length of the vagus nerve, sending up nine messages for every one it receives in return. Mediated by the biochemicals—neurotransmitters such as serotonin—that your gut produces, the nerve signals originating in your belly play an important part in setting your mood.

How does energizing your belly with movement and breath brighten your mood? I suspect that when your belly moves freely with the breath, it activates the nerve fibers that connect your gut with your brain. Your brain gets the message you're having a good time.

When you're breathing deeply, you're also increasing the supply of oxygen to your brain. Clinical research shows that regular oxygen-enhancing exercise can be as effective a treatment for depression as an antidepressant drug.

Your belly is also home to your reproductive organs and related hormones. When these hormones are out of balance they can put your emotions on a roller coaster. By stimulating blood flow and dispelling congestion, energizing your belly can help even out the ride.

Whatever nerves, molecules, or hormones may be involved, let your own experience be your guide to the mind-belly connection.

How perky do you feel when you're constipated? How playful do you feel when you've got PMS? How confident do you feel when your stomach is tied up in knots?

How do you feel following a brisk walk? How do you feel when you've given yourself room to breathe?

•

The breathing and belly work dissipated my menstrual cramps this morning. Ahhhhhh.

—Tricia

• • •

Dispense with stress
●

Unrelieved stress can lead to a variety of physical and emotional ailments. Your belly can help you to release stress. As tension dissolves, you'll feel both alert and relaxed. (If you're pregnant, see the *Practice Pointers* on p. 67.)

■

Here's how—

1• Sit or stand comfortably, or lie on your back with a pillow under your knees to ease your lower back.

2• Keeping your mouth closed, slowly inhale through your nose, expanding your belly to draw the breath in.

3• Having inhaled fully, now push your belly further out to inhale even more.

4• Then open your mouth and exhale slowly, allowing your belly to sink back toward your spine.

5• Having exhaled completely, now pull your belly further in to exhale even more.

Repeat up to ten times. Notice how tension easily fades away.

●

I incorporate belly-breathing into my daily activities to help relieve stress. It's made me more aware of myself and my body, and helped me to get in touch with my emotions and listen to my body. It's very powerful.   —Betty

Prize your powerhouse

You might think of your body as something like a machine—a collection of pumps, tubes, and gears.

You might also think of your body as a power grid, a network of connecting currents of electricity. These currents move life energy into every part of your body.

Cultures around the world have incorporated this energetic understanding of the body into their healing arts for centuries. The Asian practice of acupuncture, for example, is a systematic way to map the flow of vitality through the body and ensure that it flows fully and freely.

What moves this life force through your body? What, and where, is its source?

You guessed it: Your belly contains your life-energy battery. It's your powerhouse, hosting the generator at the network's center. It's the origin of the energy that streams through your whole body, putting the spring in your step and spreading the smile across your face.

A hydroelectric power plant needs a constant flow of water running through it in order to generate electricity. In the same way, your own powerhouse needs an abundant flow of breath in order to generate your vitality. Constrict your belly with tight pants or rigid abdominal muscles and you are significantly reducing the supply of breath to your energy generator.

Here it is again: Your physical health and emotional well-being depend on your capacity to breathe deeply. Letting your belly move with the breath allows your powerhouse to work at its peak.

•

I love feeling the instant energy. I really crave the centered, charged-up feeling that doing these belly exercises gives me.   —Patty

• • •

Words that refer to the belly actually reveal its role as our vital center. The Japanese, for example, use the word *hara* to mean both the belly and the source of life energy. In a similar way, we use "gut" and "gutsy" to mean both the belly and the soul-qualities of courage, determination, and instinctive knowing.

If something is "gutted" it has been emptied out, made powerless. When we say "Trust your gut" and "Follow your gut instincts," we're saying there's something in our bellies that we can draw upon for guidance. When we say "That takes guts" and "She's a gutsy woman," we're saying that our bellies shelter an inner source of strength.

Your belly is your powerhouse, giving you the guts to live a life you love. What could be more important?

•

Energizing my belly gives me a way, finally, to get connected to my real power any time I want to— rather than feel a little glimpse of it once every few years, then lose it and not know how to find it again.

—Sara

Hara

Hara is the Japanese word for both the belly and its soul-power. Several Japanese phrases incorporate the word, pointing to its many levels of meaning. For example—

Hara no okii hito:
>"the one who has finished his belly"
>> the fully mature person

Haratsuzumi wo utsu:
>"to beat the belly drum"
>> to lead a contented life

Haragei:
>"belly art"
>> any activity accomplished perfectly yet without effort

Hara de kangaenasai:
>"please think with your belly"
>> tap into your essential wisdom

Hara–goe:
>"belly voice"
>> a voice that expresses integrity and presence

Hara no naka wo watte misemasu:
>"a person who shows what is inside his belly"
>> one who speaks with genuine sincerity

Hara ga oki:
>"a grand hara"
>> a person who is understanding, compassionate, generous

Hara ga kirei:
>"a clean hara"
>> an honest person, one who has a clear conscience

• • •

What happens to the center...

Imagine that you and a friend are ice-skating. Your friend is facing you, standing still. You want to push her across the ice. What will you do?

If you reach out your arm and push on one of her shoulders, she'll turn but she won't cover any distance. If you put a hand on each of her hips and push on the center of her body, though, her whole body moves at once and she remains in balance.

That's the way the world works: What you do to the center you do to the whole.

Your body's center is a point within your belly, a few inches below your navel. This one point is the address for your entire self. When your belly center is the origin of your action, your whole body moves easily, gracefully, almost effortlessly. The whole of you moves as one.

Women and men around the world have named the body's center-point with words that point to its special significance. Some of these names translate as:

- Sea of Vitality
- Energy Garden
- Luminous Pearl
- Gate of the Mysterious Female
- Throne of the Creator
- Cinnabar Field

What might you name this pivotal point within your belly? Whatever you call it, remember that what happens to the center happens to the whole. Love your belly and you're on the fast track to loving your whole self.

•

I always run with my belly leading when I'm running uphill. It proves to me that the point of center, the point of power, is the belly. And when I come from that place, everything is easier and I can perform better, in any aspect of my life. —Tricia

• • •

Locating center
•

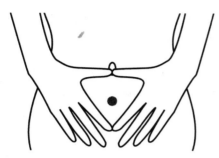

Place your palms on your belly, the tips of your thumbs touching at your navel and the tips of your index fingers touching below. Notice the triangle that your hands are framing.

Press gently yet firmly into the center of this triangle. What do you feel? Your belly center, your body's center, is here within the volume of your belly.

■

Here's another way to locate your center—

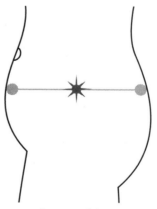

1• Sit or stand comfortably. Place one palm on your belly, your thumb at your navel. Place your other palm on your lower back, directly opposite.

2• Enter into the *Centering Breath* (see p. 19). As you breathe, imagine a string running from the center of one palm through your body to the center of the other palm. See the string, feel it, describe it to yourself.

3• Find the string's midpoint. Focus your attention at this point for several breaths. What do you observe? Notice the images and sensations that are occurring.

Gradually return your attention to your whole body and to the present moment.

• • •

Cherish the source of life

Your belly shelters your power to generate new life. Your belly is a palace of creation.

We call the Power of Being that creates, sustains, and regenerates the world by many names: God, Great Spirit, Great Goddess, and more. Is there anywhere where this All-That-Is is not?

If the Power of Being is everywhere, then it dwells within each of us. Where do you imagine this Power might choose to curl up inside your body?

•

My daughter Francie met a friend for lunch. The woman confessed: "I shouldn't be eating. I feel so fat, my belly's so big."

Francie replied: "If you found something so incredibly precious and powerful that it could bring forth *life*, how would you keep it? Wouldn't you want to wrap it in something soft and round, to cushion and protect it? That something soft and round is your belly."

—Virginia

• • •

Full-body breathing
•

Connecting your center with the whole of your body through your breath gives you a delicious, full-bodied sense of presence.

■

Here's how—

1• Sit or stand comfortably. Or lie on your back with a pillow under your knees to ease your lower back.

2• Rest your palms upon your belly, placing the center of your hands over your belly's center. Deepen your awareness into this midpoint. What do you feel here?

3• Enter into the *Centering Breath* (p. 19). As you inhale, see and feel the breath activating this centerpoint, expanding from here to fill the entire volume of your body with light, warmth, energy.

4• As you exhale, see and feel the breath returning to concentrate at your centerpoint, making it even livelier, stronger, brighter.

5• Stay with this image and sense of breathing for ten or more cycles of breath. What do you notice? How do you feel in body and mind?

Gradually return your attention to the present moment.

•

The belly-energizing practice feels balancing, integrating, and invigorating. Living with greater belly awareness makes me feel more centered, grounded, and confident..."at home" in myself.   —Patty

LIFTING THE LID

CONNECTING WITH YOUR CENTER

You've found an earthen bowl wrapped in a tattered cloth and bound tightly with metal bands. You've removed the cloth and revealed the bowl.

But its lid is stuck. A thick wax seal prevents you from lifting the lid and seeing what's inside. There is treasure inside the bowl. But how will you get to it?

Your next step is melting the seal, lifting the lid. Loving your belly, you'll be connecting with your center of being.

Loving Your Belly

Here are fifteen playful ways to create a loving relationship with your body's center.

Enjoy them, and also note: Developing a loving relationship always involves telling the truth. Many of us feel shame about our bellies, more than we might realize. We might try to ignore or minimize the hurts we've endured. Telling the truth may stir up difficult feelings, especially if you've experienced emotional or physical wounding here.

These playful ways to begin loving your belly can also be provocative. They don't substitute for professional medical or psychotherapeutic attention. If you become emotionally or physically distressed while doing any of these activities, stop and consult with your health care provider to address your individual needs.

●

At 65 years of age I have finally recognized that my "gut" isn't all "bad." I have many years of old voices and behavior to change.　　　　—Margaret

● ● ●

Bless yourself

Whatever you bless—it flourishes. Whatever you criticize—it falters. If you want to love your belly, take every opportunity you can to bless it.

Rather than ignoring your belly,
   become better acquainted.

Rather than neglecting your belly,
   notice what you're feeling there.

Rather than finding fault with your belly,
   admire its many capacities.

Rather than doubting your belly's value,
   affirm its importance to you.

Rather than worrying about your belly,
   anticipate that loving your belly will enhance
   your happiness as a whole.

Rather than blaming your belly for failing to meet
   unrealistic expectations, appreciate this precious
   source of life.

•

Every day I look in the mirror and say "What a cute belly!" Who knew such a thing was possible?!
—Kathy

Here's how—

Consider these blessings, and consider creating your own...

1• I admire my belly the way a peach blossom delights in its fruit.

2• I affirm my belly the way a sailboat speaks well of the wind.

3• I attend to my belly the way an explorer pays attention to her compass.

4• I anticipate that loving my belly will soothe me the way a mama bear nourishes her cub.

5• I appreciate my belly the way a tall tree is grateful for its roots.

• • •

Notice what you're feeling

No matter how skinny or shapely your belly might be, viewing it with a critical eye will only make you miserable.

Change your focus. Shift from criticizing how your belly looks to appreciating how it feels. Recognize that your "gut feelings" give you important information.

Yet the feelings stirring in your belly may seem vague, even uncomfortable at times. You can put words to those feelings, using images to name your belly sensations.

■

Here's how—

1• Consider this list of categories:

shoes, vessels, kitchen appliances, sources of light, types of clouds, kinds of weather, landscapes, national monuments, planets, colors, constellations, animals, flowers, fruits, vehicles, fabrics, crafts, gemstones, bodies of water, magazines, punctuation marks, sources of heat.

Add your own categories to this list.

2• The sentence below contains two blanks. Choose a category to fill in the first blank. Then fill in the second blank with a specific example of that category, saying whatever picture or word immediately comes to mind.

The way my belly feels right now, if my belly were a (category) ____, it would be a (specific example) ____.

For example, if I chose the category "flowers,"
my sentence might be:

The way my belly feels right now, if my belly were a *flower*, it would be a *red-orange tiger lily*.

Design a decoration

Design your own wardrobe of belly-celebrating underwear!

∎

Here's how—

1• Gather your supplies: fabric paints and glitter, a few paintbrushes, cotton underpants in your favorite color, a circular paper plate, masking tape.

2• Insert the paper plate into the center of the underpants to separate front from back. Fold the side edges of the undies around to the back of the plate and fasten them with masking tape so the fabric won't move as you paint on the front.

3• Enter into the *Centering Breath* (p. 19) and consider the ways in which you appreciate your belly. Let the sense of appreciation fill you fully as you take paintbrush in hand and apply a design to the fabric. You might find yourself painting a symbol that has special meaning for you or an image that has come to you in a dream.

Continue until you've created a pair of undies that honors your belly in style.

•

A woman who had had three C-sections told me: "People say I have a 'zipper belly.' I'm afraid all my innards will fall out, they'll leak all over the place."

"What does your belly need to keep all your innards contained?" I asked her. She replied, "The image that I get is my pelvis as a bowl, a porcelain white bowl with a gold rim. Even though it's porcelain, it's not breakable; it's sacred." —Lisa

• • •

Let yourself laugh

What makes you laugh so hard your belly shakes?

I saw a refrigerator magnet the other day with the words "It's called PMS because Mad Cow Disease was already taken."

I told my friend about it and we laughed. I laughed so hard my belly quaked. All the tension in my body broke up into tiny pieces and fell away.

What is a belly laugh? It's a tremor rippling through your tissues, tickling your innards. It's an inner shimmy, the cells of your body dancing with delight.

If it's been too long since your last good guffaw, now's the time to get the laughter going again.

■

Here's how—

1• Invite some friends to join you—the more, the better. Arrange yourselves on the floor so that you're lying at right angles to each other, one woman's head resting on the next woman's belly. (The first one in the chain will have her head on the floor; have a pillow handy for her.)

2• The first woman says "Ha!" The next woman adds another "Ha!" and so does the next and the next, passing the lengthening list of ha-ha's down the chain.

3• Be sure to play a number of rounds, changing places so that the first woman has a chance to be in the middle of the chain. And if you aren't all breaking up into belly laughs, start trading your bawdiest jokes!

Honor your biography

Your belly contains worlds of experience—laughter and grief, pleasure and pain, confusion and certainty, challenge and triumph. Loving your belly means learning its history.

Be gentle and respectful as you discover your belly's biography. In many ways our culture "can't stomach" woman's belly. Whether we're awake to it or not, that rejection is painful. We often cope with the culture's rejection by cooperating with it—by scorning our bellies, numbing our core feelings, and denying our instinctive knowing. We try to protect ourselves as well as we can.

When we cooperate with the culture's rejection, however, we repress our sense of self. We muffle our inner authority, guidance, and purpose. We mute our creativity. We restrict our sexual expression.

As you listen to your belly's stories and honor its biography, you create a more compassionate relationship with your belly. At the same time, you may reclaim an expanded sense of who you are.

■

Here's how—

1• What events have shaped how you think and feel about your belly? Consider the stages of your life. What did you experience as a child, a preteen, and a teenager that formed your relationship with your belly? What have you experienced as an adult?

   Jot down a quick word or phrase to note each event, listing these experiences as you remember them, whatever their actual sequence in time.

2• To stir your memory, consider—

   Beginnings:
   What was your first awareness of your belly?
   What was your first feeling about your belly?
   What's the first thing someone said about your belly?

When (if ever) did you stop breathing deeply?
    What was happening in your life at that time?
When (if ever) did you start feeling ashamed of your belly?
    What was happening in your life at that time?

Words and images:
    What have your family and friends said about your belly—
        and about theirs?
    What words have you used to speak about your belly?
    What magazines, movies, tv shows, and celebrities have
        influenced how you think and feel about your belly?

Experiences:
    What has your belly been through in relation to—
        • food, eating, mealtimes, diets, digestion, elimination
        • illness, injuries, accidents, surgery, healing
        • clothes, weight loss, weight gain, body size, body shape
        • menstruation, PMS, birth control
        • dating, sex, pregnancy, childbirth, menopause
        • exercise, sports, dance, holidays
        • creative expression
        • intuition, inner guidance, "gut feelings"

3• When your list is complete, mark each event with the year in which it occurred. Now number the events according to their sequence in time. Rewrite the list, arranging the events in chronological order—from the most distant in time to the most recent.

4• Look for the thread that links these moments in time together. Is there a theme? Is there a way in which your experience has been developing? Write a few sentences summarizing and reflecting upon what you see.

• • •

5• Look for two or three experiences that were turning points in your relationship with your belly. Develop your notes on these events further, telling the whole story. What more can you say about these events now, given your current perspective?

•

One woman recalls:

> 1st or 2nd grade: (6 yrs old) Little boy I liked elbowed me in the belly. It hurt so bad…. I couldn't breathe and just as much my feelings were hurt. We never really laughed together after that.
>
> 9-10 yrs old: My father talked about how hard my stomach was: "No flab on her." He was very complimentary about it and poked his own belly saying how it wasn't so firm anymore.
>
> 20 yrs: Very thin…until I put on a little weight in my early 20's. Nobody had ever seen me with any padding and they commented…and I felt very dowdy and unattractive and pudgy…

•

Another woman notes:

> 16 yrs. Ate so much at Thanksgiving had to lie down
> 24 yrs. First good sexual experience—very freeing
> 29 yrs. C-section; I felt torn apart

•

And another recalls:

> I've always been embarrassed about my "wub"—that's what we called our bellies in high school if they stuck out at all.

• • •

Launch a correspondence

Consider your belly to have its own identity, its own personality. You can communicate with this character by writing a letter to your belly.

The idea of your belly having its own voice, feelings, needs, and sense of humor might seem strange. If you've neglected or rejected it, you might be afraid of what your belly will tell you. Actually, you may be surprised by your belly's willingness to forgive and by the strength of its desire to create a loving relationship with you.

■

Here's how—

1• Write a letter to your belly.

2• Then write down your belly's response.

Continue the correspondence as you wish.

•

I have a powerful, gutsy belly that will lead me if I will talk and listen to her. —Susan

A woman writes to her belly:

Dear Belly-o-mine:

Creation by default: That's been our dis-connecting link. I know how much discomfort you've been in all these years. Until recently, I haven't believed that I could deliberately choose thoughts that would create something better for us both!

Well, now I know how to do better for you. Just think how much better you and I have felt in the last few months.

What do you think? Do you feel that we are creating less by default and more by consciously and deliberately choosing what is positive?

Also, now I know better what a negative or painful feeling coming from you means—it's a signal that I'm focusing on what I don't want.

Sincerely,
Ann

Her belly responds:

Dear Ann,

Boy! Have you got me full-filled with food because you haven't really known to fill me with your loving attentiveness. This is the food I need. I don't need all the second helpings and recreational tidbits. I need reasonable basics and you. You, meaning your caring attention.

But how could you ever believe that you could be that important, so important that your mere attention is so needed? But it is true whether you are prepared to believe it of yourself yet or not. I cannot go on without you, without your attention. How dare you continue believing you are not important! I am hurting and crying because you believe a lie. How long do I have to keep calling out to you while you keep saying "What? Me? How could someone be calling out to one as worthless as me? Impossible."

Well, I call out to you because you are all there is for me to call out to. I'll die without you and your attention; that makes you important to me. If you say that I don't count, that you can't be important unless you get the attention of old dead-and-gone parents, then there is no hope for me. But I have to believe the truth—that I am important because you need me and I love you.

Yours truly,
Belly

Ann writes back:

Dear Belly-o-mine,

I truly haven't thought my attention was all that important to you. Just as my inattentive parents never would have imagined how vitally important their attention could have been to me.

Not having felt valued I've found it hard to believe anything I might do or offer could matter much. And you have been crying out in neglect and I haven't believed that my attention could make any difference. Yet I'm understanding now that I can make all the difference.

How do I know? My Belly told me so.

Love,
Ann

• • •

Stay in touch

Rubbing your tummy feels good. Give your belly this gentle massage any time you want to feel calm, relaxed, and reassured.

■

Here's how—

1• Enter into the *Centering Breath* (p. 19).

2• Place your palm gently upon your navel. Slowly glide your hand in clockwise circles, spiraling outward to cover the whole surface of your belly.

3• As your hand circles, see and feel comforting light and soothing warmth penetrating deeply.

4• Still moving your hand in a clockwise direction, spiral in toward your navel. Slowly bring your hand to stillness over your navel and let it rest there for a few moments.

Enjoy the sense of relaxation you've created.

•

When on center, the self *feels* different: one feels warm, in touch, the power of life a substance like an air in which one lives and has one's being with all other things.
—MC Richards

Shield yourself in style

If you were a warrior in centuries past, your shield would serve you in several ways. As a barrier to swords and spears, it would protect your belly's vital organs from injury. Decorated with symbols invoking supernatural powers, it would frighten off attackers. Marked with signs of your ancestry, it would declare your membership in a certain tribe.

Even if you don't have to do hand-to-hand combat in your daily life, you still might want to make an abdominal shield for yourself. As you create it, whether or not you ever wear it in public, you claim your right to set boundaries, be safe, and be yourself.

If we don't shield our bellies with our self-validation, we may find that rigid abdominal muscles or an extra layer of fat is doing the job for us. As we take responsibility for protecting ourselves and envelop ourselves in self-affirmation, we no longer need that kind of armoring.

■

Here's how—

1• Gather your supplies. Choose what you will use as the base for your shield. Possibilities include posterboard, paper plates, a pizza pan, the lid of a large container.

Equip yourself with glue, scissors, colored paper, markers, crayons, glitter, stickers, pictures from magazines, ribbons, string, feathers, fabric, leather, beads, gemstones, and the like.

2• Notice whatever words and images come to mind as you consider what you want a shield to do for you. How will it serve you? When and how will it come in handy?

3• Enter into the *Centering Breath* (p. 19). Notice the words and images that come to mind as you consider:

> What protects me from injury?
> What wards off attack?
> What keeps me safe?
> What shows my courage?
> What tells the world who I am?

Let the emerging words and images guide your design.

4• When you've completed the shield's design, create a way to hold or wear it in front of your belly. Some possibilities include:

> Add a handhold to the back of the shield.
>
> Make holes in the shield's side edges and lace a ribbon through the holes in each side. Tie the ribbon behind your back and wear the shield like a low belt over your belly.
>
> Make holes in the shield's top edge. Loop a ribbon through the holes and tie the string around your waist, letting the shield hang down over your belly.

5• Wearing or holding your shield in place, go to a mirror and appreciate what you see: a woman secure in her self-validation.

• • •

Let yourself move

Take a class in African or Middle Eastern dance, Tai Chi, or any movement art that makes your body's center the origin of motion. Take a walk or put on music and dance around your living room, letting your belly lead the way. Learn and practice the belly-energizing moves in *Claiming Your Treasure* (p. 63).

Whatever you do, feel the exhilaration of letting your belly be *out there*: present, active, expressive, free. Feel the power—the "oomph"—that's been inside you all along.

•

Why is it that hardly *any* woman I know is truly okay about her size even if, and especially if, she's a twig?

That old saying is wrong: It's not that "Inside every fat woman there's a thin woman screaming to get out."

The reality is that inside *every* woman there's a fat woman trying to get out and breathe, relax her belly center. One that wants to be accepted just as she is.

Can you imagine what power and love would be unleashed if that were so? We would no longer be held back. The world would be saved! It makes my heart leap.   —Debbie

• • •

Eat in peace

Your belly's digestive organs turn food into the fuel for your life. When you eat in peace, you give your belly the time and place it needs to do this vital work for you.

Rushing through what you're eating can make your belly grumble with indignation…indigestion, that is. Taking the time to notice what you're eating helps develop your intuitive sense of what nourishes your body best. As your inner guidance becomes clear, it's easier to choose the foods that suit your individual needs, no matter what diet program may be in fashion.

Slowing down the process of eating means chewing thoroughly. Chewing your food well gets your digestion off to a good start, giving your body the nutrients it needs and promoting swift elimination.

Giving yourself a peaceful setting in which to eat enables you to distinguish hunger for food from other needs. When you're distracted, you can easily mistake many feelings—anger, fear, excitement, boredom, fatigue, sadness—for hunger. Focusing your attention allows you to know what and how much you need to truly satisfy yourself.

Begin by eating one meal or snack in peace each week. Make it a special treat!

■

Here's how—

1• Set aside ample time for preparing food, cleaning up, and then relaxing after you eat.

2• Slow down. Notice the colors and textures of the food you're preparing. Consider how this food has come into your hands. How many people and resources have played a part in bringing it to you?

3• Create a peaceful setting. Add a touch of beauty to your table with a picture, flower, candle, special bowl, soothing music—whatever pleases you. Turn off the radio or television. Sit down to eat. If you're eating with others,

• • •

make an agreement to keep conversation simple and pleasant. Arrange to address problems and conflicts after the meal.

4• Enter into the *Centering Breath* (p. 19). Notice the sensations occurring in your belly. How do you experience being hungry?

Regard the food on your plate as a gift. Savor its color, shape, texture. Bring the food towards your mouth and, even before you taste it, enjoy its aroma.

5• Place the food in your mouth, then put down your fork or spoon. Enjoy the temperature, texture, and density of the food in your mouth. Begin chewing.

As you chew, notice the strength of your jaw muscles, the motion of your tongue and lips. Notice how chewing releases the food's flavors. Enjoy the taste. How many flavors do you taste?

8• Chew until you've liquefied the food. As you swallow, feel your body receiving nourishment.

9• Notice sensations in your belly and your degree of hunger now. Are you ready for another bite?

Take a few moments at the end of your meal to appreciate the nourishment that you've created and received.

•

I no longer feel that I have a knife in my belly. If I ask my belly what it wants to eat for lunch and I eat that, it doesn't hurt. My belly's the first place where tension shows up. If I feel my stomach hurting, it lets me know that something has happened that's upset me.   —Joyce

• • •

Dialogue with your inner wisdom

If you and your belly have been writing letters to each other (see *Launch a Correspondence*, p. 41), you've already opened a channel of communication. Engaging in a dialogue makes your communication all the more immediate and intimate.

Again, the idea of speaking to your belly and listening to its reply may seem strange. Understandably, if you've ignored, criticized, or even abused your belly, you might be afraid to hear what it has to say to you. You may be surprised by how willing your belly is to create a loving relationship with you.

Activating your belly with movement and breath encourages your belly to communicate with you. You might plan to do a Belly Dialogue right after practicing the exercises in *Claiming Your Treasure*.

Write out the dialogue with your belly as it is taking place. Each party to the conversation speaks in the first person, addressing the other as "you." For example, you might say to your belly, "I wish you would…." And your belly might say to you, "I like that you…." To build a strong relationship, make a clear distinction between your voice and your belly's voice.

■

Here's how—

1• Give yourself ample time. Set aside fifteen to twenty minutes during which you'll be free from interruption. Equip yourself with a notebook or stack of paper and a pen or pencil.

Enter into the *Centering Breath* (p. 19) and notice whatever images and sensations come into your awareness as you focus your attention within your body's center.

2• Begin by inviting conversation. Your belly might not be ready to chat right away. Develop a mutual willingness to talk with something like:

• • •

"Hello! I'd really like to talk with you. Are you willing to speak with me?"

Don't be surprised if your belly is initially grumpy or skeptical. Let it speak those feelings, or let it be silent for a while as you gently repeat your invitation.

If your belly doesn't answer you at first in words, it may respond with a shift in inner sensation and imagery. Demonstrate your patience, your willingness to be with your belly and treat it with respect.

3• Make introductions. Ask your belly its name:

"What do you want me to call you?"

Use that name to address your belly throughout your conversation. One woman's belly was *Giver of Life*; another's was *Belle*.

4• Stay present. As you write, be totally honest with what's happening in the moment. There's no need to be polite, smart, or quick with this process. Express exactly what's true for you. For example—

If you're afraid that you don't know how to talk to your belly, then write:

"Belly, I'm afraid I don't know how to talk to you."

If you're worried that your belly is so angry about all the ways you've mistreated it in the past that it won't want to talk with you, then write:

"Belly, I'm worried that you're so angry with me for all the ways I've mistreated you in the past that you won't want to talk with me."

• • •

5• Express and listen to each other's feelings. Invite your belly to tell you how it feels. For example—

"Please tell me how you're feeling. I'm ready and willing to listen to whatever you have to say to me. I want to hear it all."

Invite your belly to express itself fully. When it comes to a stop, you might say:

"What else? What else do you want to tell me about how you're feeling?"

When it's your turn to express your feelings, tell the complete truth.

6• Express, listen, and respond to each other's needs. Ask your belly what it needs from you. Get the specifics. For example—

If your belly says, "I need you to be nice to me," keep asking for the details until it tells you, "I need you to sit down when you eat. I need you to turn the television off. I need you to chew your food really well."

If you can't or don't want to meet the need that your belly has stated, say so. For example—

"I don't know how to do that." Or, "That's boring. I'm not willing to do that."

You may also want to ask, "Will you help me find a way to do that?"

When it's your turn, tell the complete truth. And ask whether and how your belly can address your needs.

• • •

7• Express your gratitude to each other. Tell your belly what you truly appreciate about it. Listen to your belly appreciating you.

Make your appreciation sincere. Find something, anything, that sparks the feeling of gratitude for each of you. For example—

You might say: "Belly, with all the discomfort you've caused me, you've made me realize that I need to take better care of myself in many ways. I'm grateful to you for that."

Your belly might say, "I appreciate that you're paying attention to me."

8• Make promises to each other that you both will keep. A simple, small, very specific promise will do.

You might say, for example: "Belly, I promise that at least one day a week I will eat breakfast sitting down."

Your belly might say, "I promise I'll talk to you in this kind of conversation rather than getting indigestion to get your attention."

9• Agree—and promise—to meet and talk again. Arrange a specific time and place to continue your conversation.

Please note: Your belly needs to know that you are trustworthy. If you make a promise to your belly, plan to keep it.

If you're addressing a complex situation, you may need to engage your belly in several conversations and keep a series of promises before your belly is willing to communicate freely and fully. The way I see it, the body is incredibly forgiving. Still, if there's a history of neglect or miscommunication, your first priority is rebuilding trust.

• • •

Draw out your deepest knowing

"Trusting your gut" means using your intuition along with your logic and sense of ethics to make a choice or set a course of action.

You may be willing to trust your gut. But the guidance your belly is giving you may not come through in neat sentences or distinct sensations. Drawing the images that your belly generates can help clarify your gut instincts.

Please note: You may have been told at a tender age that you weren't creative, that you couldn't draw. If that's the case, here's good news: What you're about to do is not Fine Arts 101. If anything, what you need is a Romper Room mentality—have fun making a mess.

I use the word "drawing" as code for holding a colored marker in your hand and moving it around the paper with abandon. You won't be graded or judged. You don't have to make the page look good for anyone, not even yourself. There's no right or wrong way to do this kind of doodling. There's no such thing as a mistake. Feel your way into it, play around with it, surprise yourself.

■

Here's how—

1• Get a stack of plain white paper and a set of markers.

2• Sitting comfortably, enter into the *Centering Breath* (see p. 19). Notice whatever images and sensations come into your awareness as you focus your attention within your body's center.

3• Consider your arm to be an extension of your belly, a pipeline ready to carry information from your body's center through to your hand and out onto paper.

4• Maintaining your awareness in your belly, take the markers that appeal to you. Let your arm and hand move across the paper, spilling out colors, shapes, and lines. Give yourself all the permission you need to make your marks freely, without judgment or restriction.

• • •

5• When you sense that your drawing is complete, pause. See whether there's a word or phrase you want to add as a title or a caption. If so, add it to the page in the color and style that feels right to you.

6• If your drawing seems incomplete in some way (or you just want to do more) take a new sheet of paper and make another drawing. Allow yourself to use as much paper as you want. Give yourself full permission—to "make it ugly" or "do it wrong" or "be sloppy" or "make a mess." As you give yourself total freedom of expression, your true picture will emerge.

7• When you've finished, take a moment to regard your picture and receive its message, in the same way that you might appreciate the guidance you receive in a dream. Write the date on your drawings and keep them together in a special place.

You can do Belly Drawings before and after practicing the belly-energizing exercises included in *Claiming Your Treasure* (p. 63). Drawing a picture before you begin and again after you finish an exercise session may demonstrate the impact that energizing your belly is making on your body and mind.

If you've made before-and-after drawings, sit quietly with the two pictures in front of you, placing "before" on the left and "after" on the right. Notice how the pictures are similar, and how they differ. There's no right or wrong. What do the drawings show about the difference that energizing your belly has made for you?

Sing a proud song

Sing a song in praise of your belly with fingers snapping, hips swinging, and heels tapping.

■

Here's how—

Make up your own tune for these words, inspired by Willie Dixon's song "Built for Comfort." Or listen to Taj Mahal's rendition of the song for some musical ideas.

> Don't try to make my belly thin!
> Don't try to make my belly flat!
> You better believe my belly's *beautiful*,
> Don't you ever call me fat.
> Because I'm built for *creation*,
> I ain't built for speed.
> Well, my belly's got everything
> This woman needs.

Substitute your own words for "beautiful" and "creation" in the third and fifth lines to make additional verses.

•

After a month of struggle with intense lower back pain, job-related depression, confusion, low energy and no motivation, I woke up one morning and did my belly exercises. I felt energy, strength, and power throughout the day and into the evening.

I had been dragging myself to work and coming home feeling exhausted. Now I feel energized and alert.

I look forward to new horizons with a high charge drive coming from within. This is powerful stuff!   —Patty

• • •

Create community

Starting when you were quite young and continuing through the years of your life, you've likely been bombarded with millions of messages shaming your belly.

You know how it goes. Magazine covers blare "lose your belly" and display fashion models whose abdomens have apparently been air-brushed out of the picture. Television advertising pushes diet plans and pills. The movies make stars of women whose stomachs are pancake-flat.

The media don't mention that there are only eight supermodels in the world. Should the rest of us make ourselves miserable trying to look like them?

Yes! That's what I imagine the fashion, fitness equipment, weight loss, and cosmetic surgery industry executives are saying. Women are the ones buying their products and bankrolling their companies in the never-ending quest to make our bodies and our bellies "good enough."

When we've been set up so thoroughly to feel ashamed of our body's center, choosing to love our bellies is an act of courage. We're creating a new set of values. We're on the leading edge, exploring the frontier. We're cultural pioneers.

We can do our pioneering alone, but it's more fun to do it together. Create a belly-celebrating community with your friends and you'll enjoy each other's support.

•

My mother made me wear a girdle when I was a teenager, even though I was pencil thin. "Nothing should shake," she'd say. "Ladies don't shake."

I think that if we didn't waste our energy on worrying about our size and shape, we could move the world! —Ann

• • •

Here's a start. What can you add to the list?

1• Ask several friends to collect pictures of big, beautiful, powerful women. Paste the pictures onto posterboard, making one huge collage.

2• Watch videos that feature women of beauty and power, no matter what their size. For starters, see *Real Women Have Curves* and Queen Latifah in *Living Out Loud*.

3• Have a party to decorate your bellywear (p. 36).

4• Gather a chorus to sing praise songs (p. 56).

5• Invite a group over for belly laughing (p. 37).

6• Make stylish shields and take a group photo (p. 45).

7• Host an "eat in peace" dinner party or potluck (p. 48).

8• Take a class in African or Middle Eastern dance together.

9• Learn and practice the belly-energizing moves in *Claiming Your Treasure* together (p. 63).

10• After making agreements that provide for confidentiality and everyone's emotional safety, share your belly stories with each other (p. 38).

•

Being in a circle of women who I know and love, having time together to learn a practice to honor ourselves, I experience them and myself in many new ways.   —Sue

• • •

Wish yourself well

Send a wish for your belly's well-being.

■

Here's how—

1• Sit or stand comfortably, or lie on your back with a pillow under your knees to ease your lower back.

2• Enter into the *Centering Breath* (p. 19). Place your hands upon your belly, resting them gently over your belly's center. As you breathe, notice whatever images and sensations may be taking place within your belly.

3• Sense that your palms can actually transmit a message. You might imagine the surface of your hands emitting a light or warmth or vibration that penetrates deeply into your belly, carrying a message along with it.

4• With your own words and images, send a message all the way through to your belly's center, wishing it well. Continue transmitting your message for ten or more cycles of breathing.

As your palms send your message, notice how your belly responds. Notice any shifts in inner image or sensation. What impressions, insights, or understandings emerge for you?

• • •

VITALIZING BREATH

The *Vitalizing Breath* amplifies the energy concentrated in your body's center. Adding the power of your imagination to your process of breathing puts your mind in partnership with your body and increases your capacity to activate your vital center.

This *Vitalizing Breath* is the foundation for the breath patterns you'll find next in *Claiming Your Treasure*—breath patterns that direct source energy into expression in seven aspects of your life. The *Vitalizing Breath* is key to making the seven jewels, your inner treasure, shine. (If you have a serious medical condition, please review the *Practice Pointers* on p. 66.)

■

Here's how—

1• Sit or stand comfortably. Or lie on your back with a pillow under your knees to ease your lower back. Rest your palms lightly upon your lower abdomen. Enter into the *Centering Breath* (p. 19).

2• Locate your belly center, the point an inch or two below your navel and in toward your spine. As you breathe, begin to see and feel your belly center as a glowing sphere of radiant energy. Notice its color: Perhaps it's gold, red-orange, or ruby red. Sense its motion: Perhaps it's spinning, vibrating, pulsing, tingling.

3• As you inhale, imagine the breath entering your body through the crown of your head. See and feel the breath flowing down into your belly center and brightening the globe, making its color even more vivid. As you exhale, see and feel the breath activate the globe, making it spin, vibrate, pulse, or tingle even more.

4• Stay with these images for ten to twenty cycles of breath. Experience the sensations occurring in the core of your body and in your body as a whole.

Sanctuary

Glowing globe,
red warm belly center of me—
I soothe and comfort you,
guard and shelter.
What do I say to you?
"You are safe here
  inside."

In response
it shimmers,
it lotuses,
it galaxies into life.

       —Carol Barre

• • •

CLAIMING YOUR TREASURE
ACTIVATING SOURCE ENERGY

You've found an earthen bowl wrapped in a tattered cloth and bound tightly with metal bands. You've removed the cloth and revealed the bowl. You've lifted the lid and found the treasure waiting for you inside the bowl.

You examine each of the seven jewels in turn, admiring its color and shape. The jewels sparkle. You see they're absorbing and reflecting light from something else within the bowl, a small ruby-red sphere.

This one gem, set in the bowl's center, glows steadily. It seems to be a constant source of light. As you breathe on it, the globe brightens; the seven jewels shimmer in response.

You've found your treasure. How will you claim it and bring it into your life?

Your next step is brightening the globe in the bowl's center, illuminating the seven jewels. As you energize your belly, you'll be activating your inner source.

Energizing Your Belly

Here are seven belly-energizing moves and related breathing patterns that you can use to claim your inner treasure.

I've selected these exercises from a series of twenty-three moves that I've taught in weekly classes, workshops, and retreats for many years. For more than a decade, I've practiced the exercises daily myself. I've developed them from various styles of yoga and other movement arts. Together, these seven exercises form a well-balanced, invigorating sequence that you can easily practice in five minutes. (For detailed instruction on the original sequence, see *Resources* p. 131.)

If we were together in a workshop, I'd be teaching you these moves with enthusiasm and delight. I'd also have my eagle eye out for your comfort and safety. Since I'm not with you at the moment, use the following pointers to ensure your own comfort and safety.

I want to emphasize that, to receive the benefits of these movement and breathing exercises, you don't have to make any heroic effort. There's no need to strain. The fact is: Your body learns best when the experience is easy and pleasurable.

These moves are not about struggling to match some external ideal. They're about coming home to yourself. You don't have to go to extremes. These moves are about the pleasures of returning to center.

You can even pass on the moves and do just the breathing pattern in each section. And you can do these breathing patterns lying down. Really, what could be easier?

Enjoy!

Practice Pointers

Read and abide by these preparations and the following "do's" and "don't's." Use them to ensure that your practice is safe, comfortable, and rewarding. If you are pregnant, be sure to read the section titled *If you are pregnant*.

Remember, there's no need to strain. The beginning and end of this practice are the same: loving yourself.

Preparations:

1• Give yourself ample time, free from interruption.

2• Create a pleasant environment for yourself. Experiment with adding music to your experience.

3• Keep a journal, paper, and markers handy if you'd like to follow your practice with a Belly Dialogue (p. 50) or Belly Drawing (p. 54).

4• Wear loose and comfortable clothes—with a loose waistband, of course. Remove your glasses, jewelry, and dangling earrings to avoid injury.

5• As you begin, notice how you feel. Notice sensations in your body.

6• Focus your gaze on the picture of your heart's desire (see p. 96) or another image that inspires you.

7• Resolve to breathe fully and move slowly, investing your awareness in your experience.

Do:

1• As with any new exercise program, consult with your health care provider in advance to determine whether and how these breathing and movement exercises are suitable for you. Ask for specific guidance to address your individual needs, especially if you are pregnant or have a history of

> back, shoulder, hip, or knee injury or pain
> abdominal injury or pain
> uncontrolled high blood pressure
> asthma, diabetes, hypoglycemia, kidney disease
> heart disease, cancer, or risk for stroke

2• Warm up thoroughly before vigorous movement.

3• Move slowly and smoothly. Attend to what you're doing.

4• Move within your comfort zone; never strain, push, or force yourself.

5• Begin learning each move by practicing two or three repetitions. As you're ready, increase your repetitions to the number suggested for each exercise.

6• During menstruation, adjust your practice according to what's appropriate for you. You may, for example, prefer to practice the moves very gently and slowly during the first day of your menstrual flow.

7• Practice on an empty stomach. Allow one hour for digestion following a light meal and at least two hours following a full meal.

8• Cool down thoroughly after vigorous movement.

Do not:

1• Do not overdo. Some people might feel slightly light-headed or dizzy as the *Energizing Breath* (alone or in combination with *Bright Blessings*, *Power Centering*, *Lily*, and *Wings*) adds oxygen to the body and brain.

To avoid discomfort, at first do only a few repetitions of each exercise, and do them slowly. With practice, you'll increase your capacity to comfortably absorb abundant oxygen. As you're ready, gradually increase your practice to the number of repetitions suggested for each exercise.

2• Do not chew gum.

If you are pregnant also do:

1• Discuss with your health care provider whether and how this program might be appropriate for you, given the progress of your pregnancy and your particular health status. Ask for specific guidance in selecting and modifying the exercises to suit your individual needs.

2• Practice only the *Centering Breath* and *Vitalizing Breath*; pass on the *Energizing Breath*.

3• Practice *Bright Blessings*, *Power Centering*, *Lily*, and *Wings* with the *Centering Breath* only.

4• When practicing *Wings*, keep your feet in place to avoid losing your balance. For the same reason, keep your heels on the ground when practicing *Tree*.

Do not:

1• Don't forcefully compress your belly while exhaling.

2• Don't hold your breath for an extended period of time.

• • •

ENERGIZING BREATH

As you practice the *Energizing Breath*, you breathe in through your nose and out through your mouth. Your belly serves as a bellows, expanding to draw the breath in and pulling back toward your spine to press the breath out.

While the *Centering Breath* engages your belly in the process of breathing, the *Energizing Breath* does so even more actively.

■

Preparation:

a• Have you ever fogged a mirror with your breath as you're getting ready to clean it? Standing or sitting comfortably, place one palm in front of your mouth as if you're about to fog a mirror that you're holding in your hand. Place your other palm on your belly.

b• Fogging the make-believe mirror, open your mouth and breathe out into your upraised hand two or three times. At the same time, notice how the hand that's on your belly is moving. Most likely, it moves in toward your spine as your belly contracts with each exhalation.

c• You might notice a sound emerging as you exhale. It's simply the sound of breath passing through your throat and out your mouth. Note that you don't have to strain your throat; you don't have to force the exhalation. Your belly takes charge of sending out the breath.

Practice:

1• Sit or stand comfortably. Place your hands lightly on your belly.

2• Keeping your mouth closed, expand your belly to draw the breath in through your nose.

3• Then gently yet firmly pull your belly back toward your spine, pressing the breath out as you open your mouth and exhale. Let your throat and shoulders remain relaxed.

4• Continue with two or three slow repetitions. As you become comfortable with the practice, gradually increase to five to seven repetitions.

What do you feel happening in your belly? How do you feel in body and mind?

BREATHING VITALITY

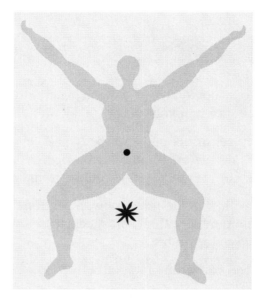

1• Sit or stand comfortably. Or lie on your back with a pillow under your knees to ease your lower back. Rest your palms lightly upon your lower abdomen. Enter into the *Centering Breath* (p. 19).

2• Locate your belly center, the point an inch or two below your navel and in toward your spine. As you breathe, picture the breath entering your body through the crown of your head, flowing down into your belly center and brightening the globe that's glowing there. Stay with this image for five to ten cycles of breath (*Vitalizing Breath*, p. 60).

3• Continue breathing in through the crown of your head, directing the breath down to and now through your belly center, breathing out through your pelvic floor and down into the earth.

4• Stay with this image and pattern of breathing for ten to twenty cycles of breath. Experience the sensations occurring in the core of your body and in your body as a whole.

• • •

Keep looking and feeling great

"Now I know why you always look like you're in love," a woman told me after moving through some belly-energizing exercises with me. She had some of the same sparkle herself.

No matter what your body shape or size is, no matter what age you are, no matter what your bone structure might be: When your energy is strong and steady, you look and feel good. You're confident. You're attractive.

As you've come to appreciate, your belly is central to your physical well-being. Your abdominal organs digest your food and eliminate waste, circulate your blood, boost your immunity.

Your belly is central to your emotional health as well. It's home to your reproductive organs and the related hormones that so powerfully affect your mood. Your belly's network of nerves contribute to relieving depression. Enabling you to breathe deeply, your belly is your best friend for relaxing and releasing stress.

Your belly is your powerhouse, your life-energy generator. Energizing your belly with movement and breath lifts your spirits and kindles the inner glow that becomes radiance for all to see.

•

For the first time I experienced fully what it means to be in touch with my belly. Now I've manifested a power which has left me with a sense of appreciation for being a woman.

My entire being, body, mind, and spirit, filled with a beauty sensed both inside and out. With each pulse I grew more beautiful. This sense of being rests with me. In connecting with my belly, I have found that I am part of a greater whole.   —Giovanna

• • •

• BRIGHT BLESSINGS •

Five repetitions, with the Energizing Breath

1• Stand with your feet parallel, hip-width apart, your knees bending slightly over your toes. Lengthen your arms alongside your body.

2• As you inhale, lift your arms up and forward to shoulder level...

3• out to your sides...

4• and up overhead. As your arms reach overhead, overlap your thumbs and fingertips, shaping a triangle.

5• Exhaling, bend your knees further and bring your hands to center, pressing lightly into your belly.

Breath & Image: Applying the *Energizing Breath* (p. 68), inhale as your arms reach forward, out, and up: You're gathering blessings from the earth, the trees, the sky. Exhale through your open mouth as your hands return to your belly: You're receiving these blessings into your body's center. See and feel a bright line linking your body's center with the earth's center, anchoring you in a strong and supportive connection.

Resting your palms over your belly center, notice and feel whatever images and sensations are occurring in your body.

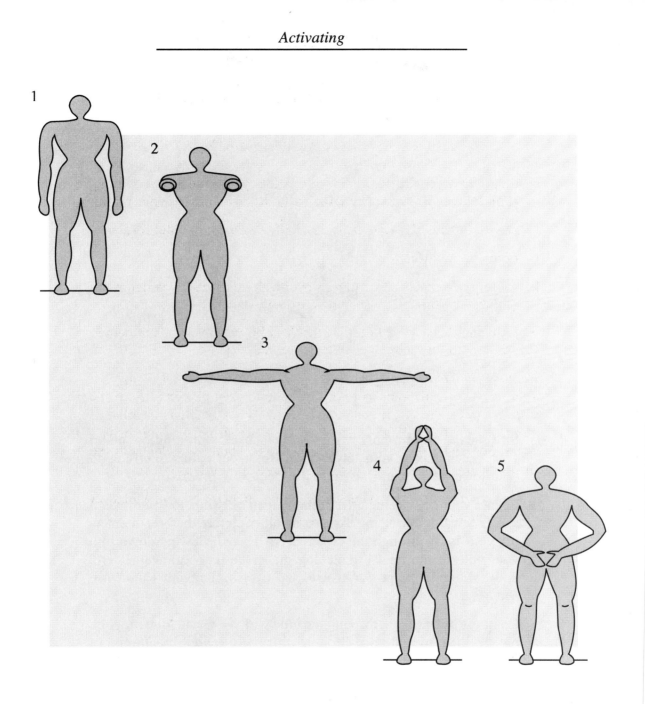

Bright Blessings

BREATHING PLEASURE

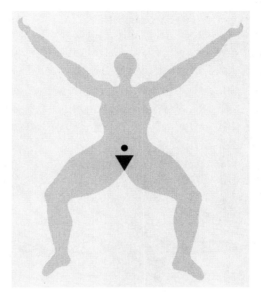

1• Sit or stand comfortably. Or lie on your back with a pillow under your knees to ease your lower back. Rest your palms lightly upon your lower abdomen. Enter into the *Centering Breath* (p. 19).

2• Locate your belly center, the point an inch or two below your navel and in toward your spine. As you breathe, picture the breath entering your body through the crown of your head, flowing down into your belly center and brightening the globe that's glowing there. Stay with this image for five to ten cycles of breath (*Vitalizing Breath*, p. 60).

3• Continue breathing in through the crown of your head, directing the breath down to and now through your belly center, breathing out through the center front and back of your lower abdomen.

4• Stay with this image and pattern of breathing for ten to twenty cycles of breath. Experience the sensations occurring in the core of your body and in your body as a whole.

• • •

Spice up your sexual pleasure

"A majority of women prefer reading a good book to having sex." As I recall it, that's what one survey discovered. When I mention this finding to friends, they nod with a knowing look.

With all the responsibilities of work, home, and family, many women are exhausted by the time they finally get to bed. More women than you might imagine mourn the loss of their interest in sex.

What is sexual pleasure? It's the play of sexual energy, one expression of your life energy as a whole. When you have more energy, you experience more pleasure.

Your belly is your powerhouse, your life-energy generator. Energizing your belly with movement and breath ignites a healthy delight in the pleasures of sex.

•

I'm claiming my wholeness as a woman that I've never had before. Energizing my belly has enabled me to gain an openness and release of sensual, sexual energy and healing. I feel increased connectedness to the feminine.   —Mimi

•

I experienced a deep, deep orgasm—and it was heightened and elongated due to breathing deeply. I realized that I was doing this deep breathing naturally. Wow.   —Tricia

• • •

• BELLY BOWL •

Five repetitions in each direction, with the Centering Breath

1• Taking a wide stance, place your feet two to three feet apart, pointing your toes outward at a comfortable angle. Keeping your knees unlocked, bend your knees directly over your toes. Keep your weight evenly distributed on your feet. Place your hands lightly on your hips.

2• Gently tilt your pelvis forward…

3• then tilt your pelvis backward; avoid overarching your lower back. Let your head and neck move naturally toward and away from your chest as your pelvis tilts forward and back.

4• Keeping your knees over your toes, press one hip forward…

5• then press your other hip forward. Notice how your knee moves further out over your toes as the corresponding hip presses forward. Let your head and neck move naturally from side to side as your hips alternate in pressing forward.

6• Still keeping your knees over your toes, roll your pelvis in slow, full circles in one direction…then in the other direction.

Breath & Image: Applying the *Centering Breath* (p. 19), inhale during one phase of the motion or one arc of the rotation, exhale during the other. As you practice this move, sense how you're stirring the liquid light of your sexual energy within the bowl that is your belly.

Coming to stillness, rest your palms over your belly center. Notice and feel whatever images and sensations are occurring in your body.

Belly Bowl

BREATHING CONFIDENCE

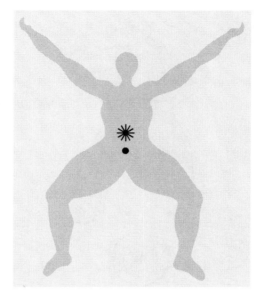

1• Sit or stand comfortably. Or lie on your back with a pillow under your knees to ease your lower back. Rest your palms lightly upon your lower abdomen. Enter into the *Centering Breath* (p. 19).

2• Locate your belly center, the point an inch or two below your navel and in toward your spine. As you breathe, picture the breath entering your body through the crown of your head, flowing down into your belly center and brightening the globe that's glowing there. Stay with this image for five to ten cycles of breath (*Vitalizing Breath*, p. 60).

3• Continue breathing in through the crown of your head, directing the breath down to your belly center, then breathing out through the center front and back of your upper abdomen at a level just beneath your ribs.

4• Stay with this image and pattern of breathing for ten to twenty cycles of breath. Experience the sensations occurring in the core of your body and in your body as a whole.

• • •

Magnify your confidence

"That took guts." Remember a time when those words could describe something you did, a time when you demonstrated courage and a "can do" attitude.

Whatever the situation, chances are that you were standing proudly, walking briskly, speaking with animation, looking directly at the person you were addressing.

You were dynamic. You showed that you were ready, willing, and able to act energetically in a purposeful way.

Your belly is your powerhouse, your life-energy generator. Energizing your belly with movement and breath enables you to draw all the more upon your inner source of strength, revealing you to be the gutsy woman you already are.

•

This practice has taken a place that has felt tight and suppressed and shameful, and spoken to that place as a mother nurtures and cradles a child, growing that child into a feeling, functional, and powerful woman.   —Joan

• • •

• POWER CENTERING •

*Three repetitions for each position of the arms,
with the Energizing Breath*

1• Taking a wide stance, place your feet two to three feet apart, pointing your toes outward at a comfortable angle. Keeping your knees unlocked and slightly bent, position your knees directly over your toes. Place your fists on your hips, palms facing upward.

2• As you inhale, reach both arms forward, twisting them so that as your hands open your palms face downward and your fingers extend forward.

As you exhale through your open mouth, bend your knees further and return your hands to your hips. Close your hands into loose fists and rest them on your hips with palms facing upward.

3• Inhaling, raise your arms and reach upward at a 45-degree angle. Exhaling through your open mouth and bending your knees further, return your hands to your hips in loose fists.

4• Inhaling, raise your arms and reach straight upward. Exhaling through your open mouth and bending your knees further, return your hands to your hips in loose fists.

5• Repeat, extending your arms upward at a 45-degree angle…

6• then reaching straight forward.

Breath & Image: Applying the *Energizing Breath* (p. 68), inhale as your arms reach out: You're reaching out into an ocean of life energy and claiming a portion of it for yourself. Exhale through your open mouth as your hands return to your hips: You're storing this energy within your body's center.

End with your palms resting over your belly center, noticing and feeling whatever images and sensations are occurring in your body.

• • •

Power Centering

BREATHING COMPASSION

1• Sit or stand comfortably. Or lie on your back with a pillow under your knees to ease your lower back. Rest your palms lightly upon your lower abdomen. Enter into the *Centering Breath* (p. 19).

2• Locate your belly center, the point an inch or two below your navel and in toward your spine. As you breathe, picture the breath entering your body through the crown of your head, flowing down into your belly center and brightening the globe that's glowing there. Stay with this image for five to ten cycles of breath (*Vitalizing Breath*, p. 60).

3• Continue breathing in through the crown of your head, directing the breath down to your belly center, breathing out through the center front and back of your chest.

4• Stay with this image and pattern of breathing for ten to twenty cycles of breath. Experience the sensations occurring in the core of your body and in your body as a whole.

• • •

Fill your heart to overflowing

What is love? Perhaps it is giving your attention and compassion freely to another, not expecting anything in return.

If that's true, then loving another goes hand-in-hand with loving yourself. Neglect yourself and it's easy to start expecting others to fill in for you.

Perhaps love is energy moving through the heart, moving with such extravagance that it fills your own heart and spills over, flowing effortlessly out to others.

Your belly is your powerhouse, your life-energy generator. Energizing your belly with movement and breath enables you "not just to love—but to persist in love."

•

The other day a friend said to me: "You talk from your guts." I like that she noticed. It's true.

What I've come to realize, with the help of this practice, is this: I am what I've been waiting for. —Mimi

•

I was tired, distressed and "down on" myself, that nasty commentator replaying negative messages over and over in my brain. After doing the belly exercises I felt empowered, centered, energized—and light. Breath of fire, of life, of joy.   —Tricia

• • •

• LILY •

Seven repetitions, with the Energizing Breath

1• Taking a wide stance, place your feet two to three feet apart, pointing your toes outward at a comfortable angle. Keeping your knees unlocked and slightly bent, position your knees directly over your toes. Close your hands into loose fists. Bend your elbows and bring your forearms together in front of your chest.

As you inhale, keeping your knees directly over your toes, bend your knees further and sink down a few inches into the beginning of a squat. Descend only to the level that's comfortable for you.

2• As you exhale through your open mouth, squeeze your buttocks together and rise into standing. At the same time, extend your arms straight out to your sides at shoulder level with your palms facing forward. Keep your knees bending slightly over your toes and avoid arching your lower back.

Breath & Image: Applying the *Energizing Breath* (p. 68), inhale as you sink down: You're reaching down into the earth to gather vitality. Exhale through your open mouth as you rise and your arms open wide: You're drawing this vitality into your belly and up through your heart.

End with your palms resting over your belly center, noticing and feeling whatever images and sensations are occurring in your body.

Lily

BREATHING CREATIVITY

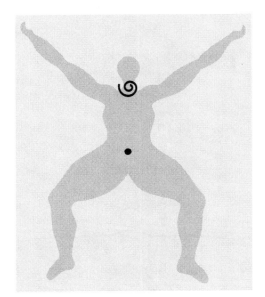

1• Sit or stand comfortably. Or lie on your back with a pillow under your knees to ease your lower back. Rest your palms lightly upon your lower abdomen. Enter into the *Centering Breath* (p. 19).

2• Locate your belly center, the point an inch or two below your navel and in toward your spine. As you breathe, picture the breath entering your body through the crown of your head, flowing down into your belly center and brightening the globe that's glowing there. Stay with this image for five to ten cycles of breath (*Vitalizing Breath*, p. 60).

3• Continue breathing in through the crown of your head, directing the breath down to your belly center, breathing out through the center front and back of your throat.

4• Stay with this image and pattern of breathing for ten to twenty cycles of breath. Experience the sensations occurring in the core of your body and in your body as a whole.

• • •

Unleash your creativity

"When I was pregnant with my children—that's when I felt good about my belly," a woman recalls. A woman's capacity to send new life into the world is magnificent beyond what words can say.

A woman's procreative power is not limited to childbirth, however. It is "pro-creative"—it is the power to promote creation in whatever dimension you choose.

Your belly is a cauldron of creative energy. You put that energy to use when you generate new kinds of relationships, new enterprises. You use it as you put your vision into action, your ideas into expression. You use it as you enfold your sense of what's beautiful and true into forms we can see, hear, taste, smell, and touch.

If you're alive, if you're breathing, you're creative. Creativity is one expression of your life energy as a whole. Your creativity flows freely as you give yourself permission and safety to express yourself.

Your belly is your powerhouse, your life-energy generator. Energizing your belly with movement and breath takes the wraps off your passion and brings forth your capacity to create.

•

This whole program has inspired so much creative work. It's a well for going down into my center and getting whatever images are there. It has helped me to go to where I just see those images.

One image that came to me was two worlds coming together, like body and spirit joining in communion. That image is an actual sculpture now.

Maybe the significance for me is that finally I'm able to bring spirit into the physical, that it's easier, there's a flow, a constant flow of energy.   —Tekla

• WINGS •

Three repetitions, with the Energizing Breath

1• Stand with your feet parallel, hip-width apart, your knees bending slightly over your toes. Lengthen your arms alongside your body.

2• If you prefer, keep your feet in place. Otherwise, bend your knees further and shift your weight onto your left foot. Inhaling, step your right foot back, keeping both knees bent and distributing your weight evenly. Keeping both hips pointing forward, press the heel of your right foot into the ground. Press the base of your spine forward to avoid overarching your lower back.

As you step your right foot back, at the same time sweep both arms forward, up, and out into the shape of a V, opening your palms toward the mid-line of your body. Look up at a 45-degree angle, gently stretching your chest and throat.

3• Exhaling through your open mouth, step your right foot forward and sweep your arms forward and down.

4• Repeat, now shifting your weight onto your right foot and stepping back with your left foot.

Breath & Image: Applying the *Energizing Breath* (p. 68), inhale as you reach your arms up and out: You're opening your wings to soar, sending forth your self-expression. Exhale through your open mouth as you step your feet together and return your arms alongside your body: You're resting in the creative power of your body's center.

Come to stillness in standing position, resting your palms over your belly center. Notice and feel whatever images and sensations are occurring in your body.

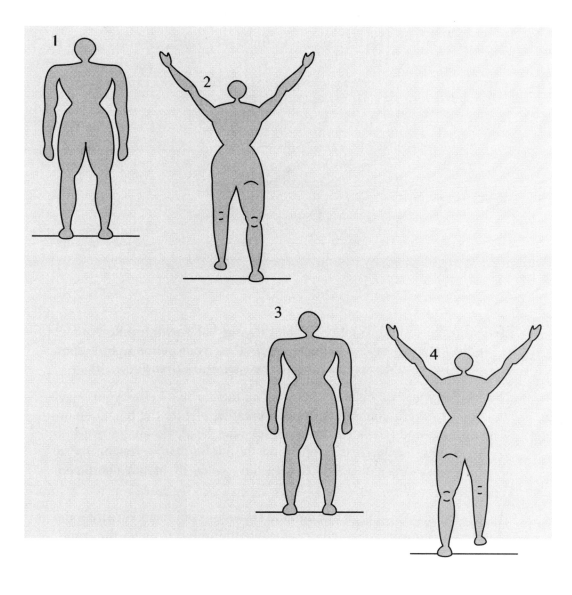

Wings

BREATHING INTUITION

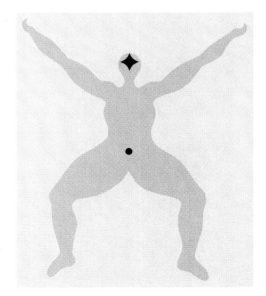

1• Sit or stand comfortably. Or lie on your back with a pillow under your knees to ease your lower back. Rest your palms lightly upon your lower abdomen. Enter into the *Centering Breath* (p. 19).

2• Locate your belly center, the point an inch or two below your navel and in toward your spine. As you breathe, picture the breath entering your body through the crown of your head, flowing down into your belly center and brightening the globe that's glowing there. Stay with this image for five to ten cycles of breath (*Vitalizing Breath*, p. 60).

3• Continue breathing in through the crown of your head, directing the breath down to your belly center, breathing out through the center front and back of your forehead.

4• Stay with this image and pattern of breathing for ten to twenty cycles of breath. Experience the sensations occurring in the core of your body and in your body as a whole.

• • •

Enhance your intuition

"Trust your gut." A friend might use these words encouraging you to follow your inner guidance. The words point to the link between your belly and your intuition.

How do you know what your gut instincts are telling you? Here are three ways my belly gives me its guidance:

> If I center my awareness in my belly and ask myself "What will happen if I...?" an image comes to mind that gives me an idea of the consequences.

> If I focus my awareness in my belly as I'm considering my options, my belly tenses up as I think of one choice and relaxes as I think of another.

> When I'm writing in my journal about an issue that's been troubling me and come to a resolution, my belly rumbles, affirming my insight out loud!

Your belly is your powerhouse, your life-energy generator. Mixed in with a multitude of hopes and fears, your gut feelings can seem to be unclear. Energizing your belly with movement and breath turns down the noise and turns up the volume on the voice of your inner knowing.

•

When I am centered in my body, I feel a solid foundation under my life. I feel as if I have an "inner guidance system" constantly at work in all decisions I make, both large and small. I know what to do.

—Connie

• • •

• TREE •

Hold each position for ten cycles of the Centering Breath

1• Stand with your feet parallel, hip-width apart, your knees bending slightly over your toes. Lengthen your arms alongside your body, your palms open to your body's midline. Focus your gaze—and your mind's eye—on a point straight in front of you.

2• If you prefer, keep your heels on the ground. Otherwise, lift your heels and roll onto the balls of your feet as one arm reaches down and the other reaches forward and up. Feel both arms rooted in your belly, stretching out from your body's center.

   Slowly lower your upraised arm as you return your heels slowly to the ground.

3• Repeat, reversing the position of your arms.

4• Repeat, raising both arms.

Breath & Image: Applying the *Centering Breath* (p. 19), gently stretch out from your center with each inhalation, lengthening upward and downward at the same time. Release the stretch slightly with each exhalation. Feel yourself being a tree, rooting into the earth and reaching up into the sky.

Come to stillness, resting your palms over your belly center. Notice and feel whatever images and sensations are occurring in your body.

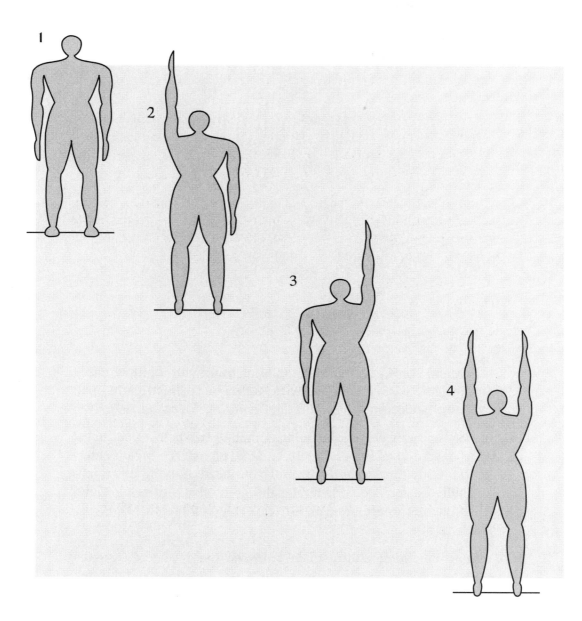

Tree

BREATHING INTEGRITY

1• Sit or stand comfortably. Or lie on your back with a pillow under your knees to ease your lower back. Rest your palms lightly upon your lower abdomen. Enter into the *Centering Breath* (p. 19).

2• Locate your belly center, the point an inch or two below your navel and in toward your spine. As you breathe, picture the breath entering your body through the crown of your head, flowing down into your belly center and brightening the globe that's glowing there. Stay with this image for five to ten cycles of breath (*Vitalizing Breath*, p. 60).

3• Continue breathing in through the crown of your head, directing the breath to and now through your belly center, breathing out through your pelvic floor and down into the earth. At the same time, breathe from your belly center out through the crown of your head and up into the heavens.

4• Stay with this image and pattern of breathing for ten to twenty cycles of breath. Experience the sensations occurring in your body.

• • •

Make your dreams come true

"Follow your heart, live your dream." You might say these words to a friend when you're urging her to be true to herself, to honor her own sense of purpose.

How do you bring your dreams into reality? You might begin by "wishing upon a star," a lovely way to image asking for heavenly help. Next you clarify your heart's desire. Then you apply your "gut determination" to bring your dream down to earth.

Your belly is your powerhouse, your life-energy generator. Energizing your belly with movement and breath empowers you to realize your heart's desire and live true to your life's purpose.

•

I have created a lot of energy with this practice. I am so much more focused and am attracting energy to me...envisioning what I want, believing it, and creating. I check in with my belly, asking her "Does this feel right?" —Tricia

•

I had been teaching art in the public schools for twelve years. Getting in touch with my belly gave me the courage I needed to let go. I said, "This is it. I need to be true to what I need to be."

After I quit, it seemed as if a burden lifted off my shoulders. Now I'm confident in running my own business. And my art is out there. —Tekla

• • •

Picture your heart's desire
•

What is your heart's desire? What do you want to be, do, and have that will make your dearest dreams come true?

When you connect your gut determination with your heart's desire, you're on your way to making it so.

Remember a time—or make one up—when you wanted something with every particle of your being. You had no doubt about it: You were totally ready to receive it. You were willing to do whatever you needed to do within the bounds of ethical behavior to receive this goodness into your life.

Recall the state of your body. How are you standing, moving, speaking, breathing? What are the sensations in your belly? What emotions are you experiencing? What kinds of excitement are you feeling? That's what I mean by "gut determination."

Gut determination is not about forcing others or straining yourself. It is about cultivating the steadfast certainty that you deserve—and are already in the process of realizing—your heart's desire.

Energizing your belly with movement and breath is one way to develop your gut determination. You can focus this power by picturing your heart's desire.

■

Here's how—

1• Get a stack of plain white paper and some colored markers. Enter into the *Centering Breath* (p. 19).

2• As you focus your awareness within your belly, let the knowledge of your heart's desire come to mind. What do you want so much you can practically taste it?

Keep breathing and focusing within your belly, waiting patiently to receive this knowing. Your heart's desire may emerge as a visual image, a phrase, or a sensation.

Check in with your belly as possibilities arise, asking your inner guidance: "Do I really want this? Am I totally ready and willing to receive this in my life?" Wait until you see, hear, or feel a mighty "Yes!" in your gut.

3• Now, with that Romper Room mentality—have fun making a mess—take markers in hand and let lines, shapes, and colors spill out onto paper, allowing an image of your desire to come into view.

Use several pieces of paper, as many as you need, to revise the image until you're satisfied it's the picture of your heart's desire.

4• You might prefer to represent your heart's desire with words rather than with a visual image. Then write a few sentences to describe what's happening and how you feel as your dream comes true. Use your favorite color and style of lettering to put these words onto paper.

5• You can place this image of your heart's desire at eye level on the wall in front of you as you practice the belly-energizing moves, using the image as your visual focus. Experiment with making each of the exercises a gesture that draws this image into your body's center; brighten the image with each breath.

As you practice *Tree*, notice how focusing your gaze on the image of your heart's desire helps you maintain your balance. As you practice *Alignment*, notice how this focus strengthens your sense of purpose.

As you sense the image of your heart's desire developing within your belly, envelop the image in your feeling of gut determination. Cultivate a sense of gratitude as well, knowing that the goodness you desire is already on its way into your life. Your clarity of purpose, your gut determination, and your gratitude bring the blessing into being.

• • •

• ALIGNMENT •

Hold each position for ten or more cycles of the Centering Breath

1• Taking a wide stance, place your feet two to three feet apart; point your toes outward at a comfortable angle. Keeping your knees unlocked and slightly bent, position your knees right over your toes.

Focus your gaze straight forward. Place your palms together at your belly center, your fingers pointing down toward the center of the earth.

2• Your left hand remaining at your belly, raise your right hand up the midline of your body to the level of your heart, now pointing your fingers up toward the sky.

3• Raise your right hand further up the midline of your body, coming to rest a few inches above your head, your fingers pointing upward.

See and feel a line of energy extending from your belly center down into the earth's center and at the same time reaching up through your heart, continuing up to and through the point where your individual spirit meets universal spirit. Feel that you are aligning your belly's power to promote creation with your heart's desire and with the grace of heaven and earth.

4• Then bring your right hand down to rest at the level of your heart.

5• Then lower your right hand to rest against your left hand at your belly center, your fingers pointing down toward the center of the earth.

6• Come to stillness, resting your palms over your belly center. Notice and feel whatever images and sensations are occurring in your body.

Breath & Image: Applying the *Centering Breath* (p. 19), see and feel the line of energy stretching through your body's core, extending further into earth and sky with each inhalation and releasing slightly with each exhalation.

Alignment

Valuing Your Bowl

Celebrating Who You Are

You've found an earthen bowl wrapped in a tattered cloth and bound tightly with metal bands. You've removed the bands, unwrapped the cloth, and revealed the bowl. You've lifted its lid and claimed your treasure. You've found the jewels inside and learned to make them sparkle.

The bowl itself may look ordinary. It might be dusty, dowdy, worn, or scarred. It's not stylish. It's not fashionable. Others may laugh at it, tell you to hide it. Still, it's your bowl and it holds your treasure. How are you going to value it?

Engendering Respect

People bring all sorts of objects to the Antiques Roadshow for appraisal. The experts look at the knife or vase and tell the owner about its history and how it was made. When the appraiser reveals the object's value, a big smile spreads across the owner's face. Hearing that this ordinary object—it might have been junk—is actually worth thousands of dollars, her face registers delighted surprise.

This ordinary earthen bowl that you've found? This belly that's been subjected to so much shame? It's not junk. It's a treasure.

I wonder how you're taking this appraisal. With shock? Delighted surprise? Skepticism? Outrage? Denial? All of these responses are understandable. Our bellies are such a sore point for so many of us. So many of us have invested our time, energy, and money in the idea that there's something wrong with our bellies and we need to fix them.

I can speak from my own experience. For twenty years, beginning when I was seventeen, I devoted myself to "banishing my belly." All I accomplished during that time was to make myself miserable and jeopardize my health. For the next fifteen years, I dedicated myself to deepening my body awareness and understanding the significance of woman's belly in the context of history and culture.

This is the truth as I know it: Woman's belly and the power it contains are necessary to our survival, both as individuals and as a tribe. What's necessary to our survival is sacred.

Dispelling the shame and learning to love my belly certainly saved my life. In the following pages I'll share my story with you; my experience may resonate with yours. I'll also share what I've learned about the sacred nature of woman's belly—how the pro-creative power we shelter in our body's center is crucial to humankind's survival, now more than ever before.

• • •

How I learned to love my belly

"Clean up your act with food, or you're going to die."

Call it intuition, call it a vision, call it a dream—that was the message I received in no uncertain terms one night. The message was literally a wake-up call, rousing me from sleep. It arrived during a time when I was in despair, still struggling with the eating disorder that had started many years before.

When I was seventeen, I made the stick-figured fashion model Twiggy my ideal of womanhood. Hoping to look like her, I'd eat nothing but cottage cheese and water for weeks at a time. My body naturally reacted to such deprivation with an uncontrollable appetite for food. Weeks of dieting alternated with weeks of binge eating. During the years that followed, the scope of my life narrowed to what I could eat, my weight, what size pants I could squeeze into. I was always on edge, always policing myself.

Eventually, I remembered a yoga demonstration I had witnessed as a teenager. Not knowing how else to help myself, I began taking yoga classes. Yoga gave me a meaningful way to nurture my body, ease my mind, and attend to my spirit. I began to live beyond obsession with my weight and shape. I began to clean up my act with food.

Deepening my practice, I trained as a Kripalu Yoga instructor and yoga therapist. As part of my training, I learned several movement and breathing exercises derived from a Japanese style of yoga. This approach to yoga focused on developing *hara*—the Japanese word for the belly as the body's physical and spiritual center, the source of our spiritual power.

The belly as the source of our spiritual power? What a concept! Here was a totally new take on the belly.

I read about the benefits of developing *hara* in Karlfried Graf von Dürckheim's *Hara: The Vital Centre of Man*. One who develops *hara*, I learned, unites with the nourishing, creative, regenerative flow of the universal life force. One who develops *hara* experiences, in Dürckheim's words, "not a power one *has* but a power in which one

• • •

stands." One who develops *hara* enjoys the list of qualities I coveted for myself: security, confidence, courage, creativity, serenity, identity, authenticity, autonomy, sense of purpose, sense of connection.

I craved these qualities. I recognized them to be attributes of the soul, expressions of a soulful life. I resolved to practice the *hara*-strengthening exercises.

To support my intention, I selected and developed twenty-three belly-energizing moves into a well-rounded workout that I've called *Honoring Your Belly*. Practicing this program, along with the inquiries detailed in *Lifting the Lid*, I entered into a whole new experience of my body's center. I no longer felt compelled to stuff or starve myself. The eating disorder gradually diminished and disappeared.

During the two decades that I was bingeing and dieting, I gained and lost twenty pounds several times each year—at least two thousand pounds in total. This repeated weight gain and loss took a physical toll, I'm sure. But even more destructive, my obsession with "banishing my belly" was dissipating my spirit, unraveling my soul. Learning to love my belly essentially saved my life.

The experience of hara

Loving my belly enabled me to experience *hara*, the source energy concentrated in my body's center. You'll experience this energy yourself, in your own way, as you practice the power-centering exercises in *Claiming Your Treasure*.

When my belly feels active and alive, I feel warmth radiating from my belly's center. Sometimes I feel a pulsing in my belly; sometimes I feel a stirring sensation, as if a small world is spinning there. Often I feel a spaciousness and satisfaction in my belly, a sensation of being full and whole.

When my belly is energized, I feel settled and content, yet also ready for adventure. I feel that I belong to the world as a whole. I'm living in the center of my world, that I'm at home wherever I go.

I experience a resonance between my body and the earth's body, a linking vibration, a mutual attraction.

• • •

Matrix Me

I am
the mother planet's
    life process.

As I plant my feet
anywhere upon her surface,

    my belly center resonates
    with my earth mother's middle.

        She rises up through me,
        our geologies join.

This earth world's center,
        be it her belly,
then my belly
        is her heart,
my heart,
        her knowing eye.

She is alive to the heat of my feeling.
She is alive to the light of my seeing.

I am alive to the words of this mother world.
I am alive to the worlds of this mother's word.

I rest in her.
The ground comes up to matrix me
And I am resting in her.

• • •

The cultural context

Understanding the significance of woman's belly in history and culture played an important part in learning to love my belly. My research led me to realize that the shame women feel about our bellies isn't ours. It doesn't belong to us.

I've heard many women say that their bellies are or have been the focus of their self-loathing. But that self-loathing is a personal response to a cultural process of invalidation. Our culture, I learned, has been devaluing women and demeaning our bellies for five thousand years.

The problem, I realized, is not with our bellies. The problem is with our culture.

I learned that attempts to degrade woman's belly—and the many forms of violence directed against women—express envy. They express the culture's envy of and desire to control the pro-creative power we hold within our body's center.

I came to understand that there's nothing inherently wrong or bad about a woman's belly. If I agree to be ashamed of my belly, then I'm cooperating with my own oppression, giving away my own power.

My research also showed that cultures in other times and places have admired woman's belly-centered power. Through myth, ritual, image, traditions of dance, and spiritual practice, these cultures have expressed their reverence for and desire to participate in this power. Feeling ashamed of my belly has no basis in reality. In fact, there's every reason to feel proud.

The role of Baubo in the Greek myth of Demeter and Persephone, the legendary search for the Holy Grail, and the practice of alchemy demonstrate three of the many ways in which cultures around the globe have celebrated woman's belly and the pro-creative power we shelter in our body's center.

The belly goddess

In myth, ritual, and sacred image, woman's belly is a goddess.

The ancient Greeks named their belly goddess Baubo and gave her the pivotal role to play in Demeter's search for her daughter. Baubo makes the difference between the life and death of the world.

This is the story: Hades has raped and abducted Demeter's daughter Persephone, taking her away to his underworld realm. Demeter—also known as the earth goddess, Gaia—is devastated. The earth reflects her despair in fields that are barren, crops that cannot grow. Famine threatens human survival.

Demeter arrives at the place called Eleusis, nearly immobilized by grief. Baubo comes to stand before her. She tells bawdy jokes, dances a hip-wiggling jig, lifts her skirt, and flashes her vulva.

Baubo's rowdy antics make Demeter laugh and laugh. Seeing Baubo bare her belly, Demeter remembers who she is and the power that she holds.

The belly laughter that Baubo provokes dispels Demeter's depression and restores her will. Now Demeter has the guts to continue looking for her daughter. She eventually finds Persephone and the earth becomes fertile again, saving humankind from extinction.

The ancient Greeks enacted this story annually in the Eleusinian Rites, a secret initiation. The details of the ritual remain a mystery. What is known, however, is that those participating in the ritual lost their fear of death. In some manner, they received a taste of eternal life.

The belly goddess personifies—deifies, really—the power of life to reach beyond death. She is the life-restoring force not only in the Greek story of Demeter but also in the Egyptian myth of Isis and in the Japanese myth of sun goddess Amaterasu. The belly goddess figures in the stone carvings that ornament English and Irish churches, European cathedrals, and Indian temples. She appears in Eastern European embroidery and in motifs that have appeared for thousands of years in Africa, Asia, the Pacific islands, and the Americas. Such images are kin to the engravings that our earliest ancestors etched into cave walls.

The belly goddess, in her many names and guises, lives in the origins of human consciousness. She is the sacredness of woman's belly.

• • •

The Holy Grail

In some legends, the Holy Grail is the cup from which Jesus drank at the Last Supper. In others, it's the cup into which Joseph of Arimathea collected Jesus' blood as he died on the cross.

Possibly, it's a set of documents that prove Mary Magdalene was the wife of Jesus and the mother of their child. Perhaps it's a reliquary containing Mary Magdalene's remains.

The Holy Grail—*San Graal* in Old French—might refer to Mary Magdalene herself. The Grail, then, is the emblem of her pregnant belly as she carried Jesus' royal blood—*Sang Raal*—into another generation.

Whatever the Holy Grail might be in legend or fact, it's often pictured as a stemmed cup—a chalice—signifying the source of life everlasting. The quest for the Grail is the quest for eternal life.

The form of the chalice is its meaning. The geometric proportions that shape the chalice are the same as those that locate the body's center within the length of the human body. The basis for these proportions, in both chalice and body, is the square root of 2.

From ancient times to the European Renaissance, artists and architects incorporated the numerical relationships found in nature into their designs. They perceived that the proportions ordering the natural world revealed universal principles. Embedding the same proportions into their constructions, they imbued their own work with sacred meaning.

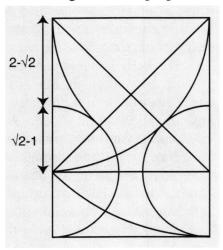

What is the significance of the square root of 2? The square root of 2 (also written as √2) is the single number which, when multiplying itself, produces the number 2. It is the one number which, of itself, produces doubling.

The essential meaning of √2 is regeneration. The root of 2 is the root from which life proceeds.

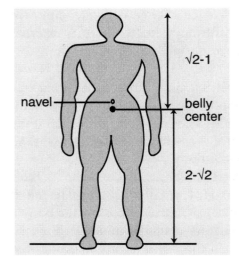

Given the geometry of its form, the chalice is a visual code for the self-generating source of life. At the same time, it's a code for the life force located in the body's center.

The Holy Grail signifies the pro-creative power that Mary Magdalene and all women shelter within our bellies. The Holy Grail is every woman willing to carry the sacredness of life into yet another generation.

•

When my daughter was a toddler, when she met someone for the first time, she'd lift her shirt up and show them her belly.　—Tori

Alchemy

Although it became the basis for the science of chemistry, alchemy was originally a spiritual practice. Transforming matter in the external world, alchemists intended to produce an internal, personal transformation as well.

As alchemists worked in Asia, Africa, and Europe, their goal was to create an elixir of immortality, a substance that would bestow healing, youthfulness, life beyond death. The crucible in which they attempted to produce this substance, the *menstruum universale*, was the *vas spirituale*, symbolizing the sacred womb.

Chinese alchemists used the bright red metal cinnabar as their starting point in changing matter from one form into another. The metal names the belly's centerpoint as well: The Chinese word for the body's center, *tan tien*, means "cinnabar field" or "cinnabar mine."

Manifesting the Inner Child

In the practice of Chi Kung, the belly is the "alchemical crucible." Breathing patterns refine the circulation of *chi*, the life force, and engender an "immortal fetus" or "immortal child." The 17th century Chi Kung classic titled *Pointing to the Meaning of Spirit and Body* illustrates a man sitting in meditation, a child developing within his body's center.

Using the image and potency of woman's womb as a guide, alchemists working both internally and externally were seeking to replicate the pro-creative power concentrated within a woman's belly. They were seeking to replicate the self-generating source of life.

• • •

Tribal survival

What's necessary to our survival is sacred.

To our ancestors, it was obvious. The tribe's survival through time depended upon women's capacity to bear and raise healthy children. The pro-creative power dwelling within woman's belly granted life beyond death.

The language of our ancestors bears witness: The ancient Hebrew word for "tribe" also means *mother*. The word for a clan within the tribe, *batn*, also means *belly*. Woman's belly makes us kin. Woman's belly defines and sustains our community.

The wisdom and power that we carry within our body's center is ancient. I can feel it threading back to the origins of life on this planet. The wisdom and power that we carry within our body's center is the instinct for self-preservation.

This instinct for self-preservation speaks to us through our gut feelings. This instinct is the power that urges us through sex and child-birth. This instinct is the force that moves us to fulfill our soul's purpose. This instinct is the energy that connects us with humankind and with all of earth's creatures.

Today, humankind's survival does not primarily depend upon women's capacity to bear children. It depends upon the conditions into which our children are born. What endangers the tribe's survival now is war, famine, poverty, injustice, disease, and environmental destruction.

But the tribe's survival still depends upon woman's belly. Our pro-creative power is not just for making babies.

•

If nonviolence is the law of our being,
the future is with woman. — Gandhi

• • •

In Gaia's lap

Yesterday, near dusk, I took a walk through the woods and afterwards lay on my back on a grassy lawn. A ridge of blue mountains rimmed the horizon. As my spine stretched out upon the ground, it seemed to tingle with sensitivity, ready to receive communication.

I wondered: "What does the earth have to say to me? I'll listen." Immediately, I sensed a voice rising, saying: "Save me! Save me!" I turned over then, touching belly to earth and felt a faint heartbeat.

What are the dimensions of the ecological crisis occurring across this planet? Scientists predict that we'll make the planet uninhabitable in the foreseeable future. Historian Roger Launius says global destruction is inevitable:

> Ultimately we're not going to be able to survive on this planet. We have to become a bi-planetary, tri-planetary, multi-planetary species if we have any hope of survival.
>
> Somewhere out there, there's an asteroid with our name written on it. We may do something to our environment to make it impossible to survive here. If we want to survive as a species, we have to move beyond this planet.

How do you feel reading these words? What do you feel in your belly? I feel outraged. Reading those words is gut-wrenching. Global disaster is a stark proposition, hard to digest, tempting to deny. What could any of us possibly do to avert such a catastrophe?

Deep Ecology activist John Seed says that the rate of environmental destruction is so rapid that, unless we spark "an unprecedented revolution in consciousness," no action that we take now can save us. "Nothing but a miracle would be of any use," he declares.

I believe women—you, me, all of us—are the miracle.

What do you imagine would happen if women acknowledged the pro-creative power we carry within our body's center? We would know indisputably, in our guts, that our bodies are earth's body. What degrades the earth damages us. What nourishes the earth nurtures us.

· · ·

When we love our bellies we open to a tender, intimate connection with the planet. As we allow ourselves to breathe deeply, we notice the quality of air. As we allow ourselves to eat in peace, we notice the quality of food and we care about the soil in which it grows. As we feel our kinship with the trees, we notice the fate of the forests.

We have been sitting in Gaia's lap for a long time. Now it's time for us to hold her in ours.

As we obsess about our body weight and shape, we bankroll the cosmetic surgery and weight loss industries with more than $40 billion each year. What else could we do with our $40 billion?

What do you imagine would happen if, instead of trying to banish our bellies, we directed our core energy and our money to healing the distress within our communities, nations, the world? What would happen if, instead of trying to shrink our stomachs, we used the resources we already have to ensure humankind's survival?

What do you imagine would happen if women took charge of our pro-creative power, claimed it as our own?

•

For nearly two years my grandmother had been coming to me in my meditations. I knew she was bringing a gift for me, but for eighteen months I wouldn't even look at what she was holding. When I was willing to look at it, I saw that she was holding a gold ball of energy. After another few months, I took the ball from her and I brought it into my belly.

After that, everything fell into place. A community development foundation asked me to be its director. I accepted the job once the Board agreed to my plan for genuine grassroots empowerment.   —Linda

• • •

We would discover that we already possess the courage, confidence, passion, compassion, creativity, and insight that we need to act on behalf of the earth and all her creatures.

For millennia, women have expressed our pro-creative power by bearing and raising healthy children. Our pro-creative power has always worked through us to ensure the survival of our lineage, our family, our tribe. The birth-giving capacity of our bellies has ensured the survival, and evolution, of the human species.

In these times, our tribe is all of life. Our home encompasses all of earth. Today, women have the opportunity—perhaps the calling—to apply our pro-creative power to preserving life on this planet.

Imagine: We cultivate and direct our pro-creative power to generate peace, justice, and ecological sustainability within every realm of human endeavor.

Imagine: We bring our pro-creative power to bear as we establish new ways to feed, shelter, educate, employ, entertain, inspire, and govern ourselves. We organize new ways to promote our health, resolve our conflicts, serve each other, protect each other, and preserve the life of the natural world.

Where do we start? We start with ourselves. We value and validate ourselves. We celebrate our body's center as the chalice of our sacred wisdom and spiritual power.

And we dance with the belly goddess, indulging in a regular dose of belly laughter. We add another chapter to the story of Persephone, Demeter, and Baubo:

> In the previous episode, Hades abducted Demeter's daughter Persephone, raping and taking her to his underworld realm. With Baubo boosting her courage, Demeter continued searching for Persephone until she found her. Retrieving her daughter, Demeter restored fertility to the earth and allowed humankind's survival.

• • •

In this episode, Hades is more subtle. He captures Persephone's attention with gilded trinkets and rhinestone jewelry.

He also gives Persephone a mirror. The mirror is warped; it distorts her image whenever she seeks to know her own beauty. The mirror captivates Persephone, totally absorbing her in a never-ending effort to fix how she looks.

Meanwhile, Demeter has been poisoned, robbed, battered. She's sick; her vitality fades daily. The earth suffers: The air is foul, the rivers are toxic, the soil is barren, the oceans are dying. Industrial pesticides, pollutants, and pathogens aggravate Demeter's chronic illness. They begin to penetrate her daughter's body and sicken Persephone as well.

Now is the time to beckon Baubo into the story. Let's ask Baubo to wake Persephone from her trance and take her to Demeter.

Persephone sees that the earth goddess is near death. She understands that Demeter's illness heralds her own demise. She alternates between denial and despair.

Then Baubo, with her bawdy jokes and hip-wiggling jigs, brazenly reminds the woman who she is. Flashing her belly, Baubo reminds Persephone that she holds sacred power within her body. Emboldened to act bravely, the woman...

How do you say the story goes from here?
I'll leave you with this prayer:

> May we know ourselves to be sacred beings.

• • •

• • •

APPENDIX

OUR HISTORY, OUR FUTURE

For five thousand years Western culture has attempted to control, exploit, and usurp the pro-creative power that women shelter within our bellies. In the following pages you'll find some of the ways in which our culture has worked its violence against women and our body's center.

In our effort to avoid the culture's violence, many women—myself included—have internalized its animosity. We've targeted our bellies and inflicted injury upon ourselves. In the following pages you'll also find some of the ways in which we've made the culture's oppression our own.

This information is not pleasant. I include it because I must. I must acknowledge the enormous suffering that women have endured and still do. Our culture attempts to steal away our soul-power and invalidate our center of being. Our culture attempts to deny us our sense of self and the opportunity to be who we fully are. The pain of living in such a culture is great.

My intention in presenting this information is not to blame others or ourselves. My intention is not to cast women as victims or bimbos.

My intention is to indicate the magnitude of the courage and compassion we must have for ourselves and each other as we enter into loving our bellies. With such courage and compassion, we can reclaim our central power and use it to serve our greatest purpose.

Our history, our culture

In the process of learning to love my belly, I had to ask: What is the significance of woman's belly in history and culture? I needed to develop a broader understanding of the shame that I felt with respect to my belly. I needed to replace shame with compassion.

Asking that question led me to the beginnings of human experience. I learned that our ancestors imaged the ultimate Power of Being in the form of a woman—the Great Goddess, Mother of the Universe. They understood the world as the body of the Sacred Feminine. The art that our ancestors made, beginning with the outline of vulvas etched into cave walls, honored the pro-creative power of woman's belly. Our ancestors understood woman's generative power as kin to the power creating, sustaining, and regenerating the world.

My research demonstrated that, through history, women's standing within a culture has correlated with that culture's respect for woman's belly and regard for the Sacred Feminine. The last five thousand years of Western civilization has degraded woman's belly, women, and the Sacred Feminine—as well as native peoples, nature, and the feminine sensibility within men—in a single process of devaluation. (Even when big bellies were in vogue in Europe, the shape of a woman's body was serving a man's convenience. A woman's round belly was a sign that her husband was wealthy; it added to his prestige.)

Our culture, I learned, subjects woman's belly to both overt and covert violence. The modern methods of disempowerment include incest and rape, assault upon pregnant women, unnecessary hysterectomies and Caesarean sections, restrictions on women's authority in pregnancy and childbirth, and reproductive technology.

My study of cultural violence against women and woman's belly was gut-wrenching. It was also liberating. I recognized that, whatever shame I might feel with respect to my belly, the shame wasn't my idea—it was culturally imposed. The shame was only mine if I chose to make it so.

And, with compassion, I recognized the courage it requires, within this history of violence and culture of degradation, for any woman to love her belly. Loving our bellies—truly loving ourselves—takes guts.

• • •

Woman's belly as a target of assault:

- In Europe, from the 15th through the 17th centuries, church and state put an estimated six million women to death. During the "witchcraze," the Inquisition slaughtered midwives, herbalists, and healers—women who possessed the traditional knowledge and skills for sustaining women's pro-creative power.

  The Inquisition's executioners hung, burned, and tortured women. One method of torture was forcing water down a woman's throat, then beating on her bloated belly until her internal organs burst.

- A woman is raped in the United States every six minutes.

  In the 1990s, Serbian soldiers raped 20,000 to 50,000 Bosnian women, ranging in age from six to seventy years old, as an element of military strategy.

- In the United States, as many as 25% of pregnant women are battered by their partners; 40% of assaults on women begin during the woman's first pregnancy. Pregnancy doubles a woman's risk for being battered.

  Murder is the leading cause of death among pregnant and recently pregnant women.

- Hysterectomy is the second most common major surgery performed upon women in the United States. More than 600,000 hysterectomies are performed in the United States each year, costing more than $5 billion.

  At least 70% of the hysterectomies performed in the United States are unnecessary.

  More than one-fourth of all American women will have had a hysterectomy by the age of sixty.

• • •

- Caesarean section—surgical removal of the baby from a woman's uterus—is the most common major surgery performed upon women in the United States.

- At least 22% of women in the United States are giving birth by Caesarean section.

- The rate of Caesarean deliveries has been increasing among all women, including women in first pregnancies with healthy babies in the correct position for birth.

- While Caesarean sections can be life-saving operations for both mothers and babies, unnecessary procedures more than triple the risk of death during childbirth and increase the risk of post-delivery infection.

Woman's belly as a resource to exploit:

- As the Inquisition executed more than six million European women—midwives, herbalists, and healers— it also eliminated common knowledge of methods for promoting childbirth, contraception, and early abortion. Women lost both the knowledge and authority to regulate their own pro-creative power. Unlimited reproduction served to populate colonies, armies, factories, and markets. As the Industrial Revolution proceeded, worldwide population increased rapidly.

- In the United States, from the 19th century through the first decades of the 20th century, educating women to take charge of their pro-creative power was illegal. Information about preventing conception—even about preventing venereal disease—was deemed to be obscene. Making such information available was punishable by a thirty-year prison sentence.

- Nearly half of all pregnancies in the United States are accidental, including more than 30% of pregnancies occurring among married couples. Yet organizations of church and state attempt to reduce access to contraception, sex education, and abortion.

43% of women will have an abortion by the time they are forty-five years old.

Before abortion was legalized in the United States, at least 5,000 women died annually in illegal abortions.

The legalization of abortion in the United States nearly eliminated all deaths due to the procedure.

- Reproductive technology—including artificial insemination, embryo transfer, *in vitro* fertilization, the use of surrogate mothers, gender determination favoring male fetuses, and cloning—industrializes the birth process, removing it from the context of women's authority.

Reproductive technology compensates for—and serves to mask—the increasing infertility among women and men corresponding to the prevalence of industrial pollutants and pathogens in our environment.

Woman's belly as an object to control:

- A law in Norfolk, Virginia requires a woman to wear a corset while dancing in public. If she dances without wearing a corset, or if she adjusts it while she's dancing, the authorities can shut down the dance hall.

Compressing the abdomen, shortening the breath, and causing abdominal muscles to atrophy, corsets seriously diminished women's vitality through the 20th century, serving as instruments of social control.

• • •

Cosmetic surgery:

- Approximately 80,000 women buy tummy tucks each year. Women are expected to spend more than $350 million on surgically shrinking their stomachs annually.

Self-mutilation:

- In Lauren Greenfield's *Girl Culture*, one photo shows a girl cutting her belly: That is where her uterus is, that's how it hurts to be a woman. As Greenfield notes, "The girls who do it talk about wanting to bring their pain and their scars to the outside, making them visible."

Dieting:

- Americans spend more than $40 billion on dieting and diet-related products each year.

- Most fashion models are thinner than 98% of American women; 80% of women are dissatisfied with their looks.

- 50% of American women are dieting on any given day.

- 80% of American girls have started dieting by the time they are ten years old.

- Dieting drastically increases a teen girl's chance of developing an eating disorder.

Eating Disorders:

- In the United States, five to ten million girls and women have eating disorders. Eating disorders are on the rise among women in midlife.

- Anorexia is a leading cause of death among young women. Five to ten percent of anorexics die within ten years of the eating disorder's onset due to related causes, including cardiac arrest and suicide.

Our future, our choice

Western culture has been brutal to women, targeting our bellies with many kinds of violence. Such treatment has made woman's belly an uncomfortable place in which to be.

Accordingly, so many women—myself included—have tried to flatten our bellies and hide them from sight. We hope that by removing the target we'll avoid the abuse. We try to comply with the culture's conventions. Like hostages becoming loyal to our captors, we cooperate with our own oppression.

But when we make our bellies rigid, we cut ourselves off from our core energy, our pro-creative power. We make our body's center the focus of our self-contempt. We unconsciously work the culture's violence upon ourselves.

The culture entices us to become agents of our own disempowerment. It tempts us to enforce its restrictions upon ourselves and each other—with diet foods, cosmetic surgery, Barbie dolls, and instant-slimming undergarments.

The culture constantly bombards us with directives to belittle our bellies. But the good news is:

We do not have to torture ourselves any longer.

We don't have to make the culture's cruelty our own. We don't have to enforce its oppression upon ourselves, our friends, our daughters, our sisters.

We can choose to honor our body's center, our center of being. We can ungirdle our bellies and let ourselves breathe, and feel. We can honor and express the power that we already carry within us.

As we learn to love our bellies, we can consider ourselves to be cultural pioneers. In every moment that we honor our bellies we are revaluing and reconsecrating our womanhood. We are transforming our culture. We are creating a new world.

• • •

Dialogue with my belly

Belly, this book is almost finished. Is there anything else you want to tell the women?

> Tell them there's nothing to fear. Tell them the story of "Pandora's Box."

Tell it with me?

> You start, and I'll chime in.

As we hear it these days, "Pandora's box" means something that lets all manner of hell break loose when you look into it. Trouble, hardship, problems, difficulties all rise up and come at you. You wish you'd never opened up the subject, never looked into the box to begin with.

The story of Pandora's box, as recorded by the Greek poet Hesiod in the 8th century BCE, goes like this:

Zeus gave Pandora, a mortal woman, to Prometheus to be his wife. For a wedding gift, Zeus and his buddies gave Pandora a beautiful box and told her not to open it.

> What a set-up!

Pandora opened the box anyway. Out flew war, pestilence, famine—all the ills and evils besetting humankind. She couldn't shut the lid fast enough to stop them from escaping. But one thing remained at the bottom of the box. What remained was hope.

> Pretty wimpy.

As you see, this story blames women for all the troubles of the world.

> What a low blow.

• • •

You said it.

What's the story on this story?

The story as we know it actually contains an error in translation. When Erasmus was translating the text from Greek into Latin in the 16th century, he took the word *pithos*, meaning "vase," for the word *pyxis*, meaning "box." Pandora's vase became Pandora's box.

What's important about that?

For ages, the vase has been a symbol of woman's womb, the belly's capacity for birth and regeneration. Pandora was not a ditz. Nor was she a mortal. *Pandora*, meaning "All-Giver," was another name for Rhea, Great Goddess, Mother of the Universe—the Power of Being imaged in female form.

"Pandora's box" was originally Rhea's vase, meaning her womb. Rhea's vase signified the source of all life.

The story of "Pandora's Box" is one example of Western culture's process of demeaning women and our body's center. The story devalues woman's belly, taking it from sacred to shameful.

A woman's belly is not "Pandora's box"!

Woman's belly is Rhea's vase. There's nothing to be afraid of or ashamed of with respect to our bellies. We have every reason to feel proud. Our bellies are awesome.

Yes!

This is what I know: Reverence for woman's belly goes back to the beginning of time. Now, as always, our pro-creative power is the possibility for human survival. Woman's belly is the sacred source of life.

• • •

Notes

Welcome

p.2 • *Woman's Belly Book.* Since this book draws on my experience as a woman, I'm writing to and for women!

p.3 • *Breeding for non-being.* Daly.

Finding treasure

p.5 • *Seven jewels.* The "jewels" correspond to the seven major *chakras*, spinning wheels of energy aligned along the body's midline, defined in the study of yoga. For detailed discussion, see Brennan, Judith & Vega.

p.7 • *Protective padding.* Genelli.

p.9 • *Path of self-love and acceptance.* Personal communication, Alison Hilber, August 2003.

Unwrapping the Gift

p.13 • *Refuse to wear.* Annie Lamott, "Let Us Commence," speech at UC-Berkeley, May 2003.

p.14 • *The genes for a fat-free midriff.* Ruiz.

p.14 • *Round bellies...in vogue.* Hollander, Steele.

p.14 • *Power of woman's belly.* Gadon, Gimbutas, Noble.

p.15 • *Robust visual reminder.* Chernin.

p.15 • *Zip code of the soul.* Personal communication, Jeanette Stokes, director of Resource Center for Women in Ministry in the South, December 1997.

p.19 • *Centering Breath.* If you have a serious medical condition, consult with your physician to ensure the safety of even this breathing pattern for you. Abdominal breathing may not be suitable, for example, if you have hypoglycemia, diabetes, or kidney disease. For an excellent discussion of abdominal breathing and hyperventilation, see Cohen, Chapter 9, Healthy Breathing.

p.20 • *Sleep easy.* Yamaoka, pp.30-31.

p.21 • *Nerve signals originating in your gut.* See E A Mayer et.al., "The evolving neurobiology of gut feelings" in E A Mayer and C B Saper, eds., *The Biological Basis for Mind Body Interactions.* Amsterdam: Elsevier, 2000, pp.197-206. Also M D Gershon, *The Second Brain.* New York: Harper Collins, 1998 and personal communication, July 2003.

p.21 • *Nerves that connect your gut with your brain.* Stimulating the vagus nerve relieved depression among patients with major depression; see H A Sackeim et.al., "Vagus Nerve Stimulation for Treatment-Resistant Depression," *Neuropsychopharmacology,* vol. 25, no. 5, November 2001, pp.713-728.

p.21 • *As effective a treatment for depression.* See M Babyak et.al., "Exercise treatment for major depression," *Psychosomatic Medicine* vol. 62, no. 5, pp.633-638, September 2000.

p.22 • *Dispense with stress.* Yamaoka, pp.29-30.

p.23 • *Practice of acupuncture.* See Matsumoto & Birch for a thorough discussion of *hara* in healing arts.

p.23 • Hara...*Japanese word.* Dürckheim, Yamaoka.

p.26 • *Sea of Vitality.* Ellis.

p.26 • *Energy Garden.* Personal communication, Dennis McCarthy, November 2002.

p.26 • *Luminous Pearl.* Cohen, p.127.

p.26 • *Mysterious Female.* Cohen, p.342.

p.26 • *Throne of the Creator.* Waters, pp.10-11.

p.26 • *Cinnabar Field.* Cohen, p.342; Ellis.

p.29 • *Full-body breathing.* Masunaga, pp.48-51.

Lifting the Lid

p.33 • *Whatever you bless.* King.

p.37 • *Magnet.* Claire Vohman, www.clairewashere.com.

p.37 • *Ha-ha's.* See Andrew Fluegelman, ed., *More New Games & Playful Ideas.* Toronto: Doubleday, 1981.

p.38 • *Belly's stories.* Progoff, Rainer.

p.44 • *Gentle massage.* Chang.

p.50 • *Dialogue.* Progoff, Rainer.

p.56 • *Built for Comfort.* Taj Mahal's performance of Willie Dixon's "Built For Comfort" is collected in his CD set *In Progress & In Motion,* Sony, 1998.

p.57 • *Only eight supermodels.* Hilber.

Claiming Your Treasure

p.83 • *Not just to love—but to persist in love.* Sue Monk Kidd, *The Secret Life of Bees.* New York: Viking, 2002.

p.98 • *Alignment.* See Brennan, Chapter 17, Our Intentionality and the Hara Dimension; Claremont de Castillejo, p.137; personal communication, Tokiko DeSola, July 1997.

Valuing Your Bowl

p.102 • *Antiques Roadshow.* Produced by WGBH-Boston for public television. On program #710, a young woman brought in a bronze statue her grandmother had bought at a yard sale. The appraiser valued the 19th century sculpture of Thetis, a goddess intent on protecting her son with divine armor, at $4,000-$6,000. Hearing the object's value, the woman's eyes widened; she had been using the sculpture as a doorstop.

p.103 • *Japanese style of yoga.* Oki.

p.106 • *Culture's envy....* Samuel Johnson, one of 18th century England's most influential figures, put it plainly: "Nature has given women so much power that the law has very wisely given them little." Letter to John Taylor dated August 18, 1763 in R W Chapman, ed., *Letters of Samuel Johnson,* vol. 1, 1719-1774, Oxford: Clarendon Press, 1952, p.157.

p.107 • *Belly goddess.* Estés, Chapter 11, Heat: Retrieving a Sacred Sexuality; Hall; Lubell.

• • •

p.107 • *Eastern European embroidery.* Kelly.

p.108 • *The Holy Grail.* Starbird; also Dan Brown, *The Da Vinci Code.* New York: Doubleday, 2003.

p.110 • Vas spirituale. Walker, p.422.

p.110 • *Alchemical crucible.* Cohen, p.342.

p.110 • *Immortal child.* See image captioned "The Inner Child Manifests," Cohen, p.126. Drawing after an illustration captioned "Tao alchemy births the 'immortal child' that lives within each of us." *Chi Newsletter*, Dao Alchemy Research Institute, Spring 2003.

p.111 • *Hebrew word.* Walker, p.331.

p.111 • *Nonviolence...woman.* D G Tendulkar, *Mahatma.* vol. 3, 1960, p.33.

In Gaia's Lap

p.112 • *In Gaia's lap.* The Maryland Womyn's Festival.

p.112 • *Roger Launius.* "NASA Past and Future," *Weekend Edition-Sunday*, National Public Radio, July 20, 2003.

p.112 • *John Seed.* Recorded in *To Wake Up One Day Different*, Video Project, 1996.

Appendix

p.118 • *Our history, our culture.* Baring & Cashford, Daly, Eisler, Gadon, Gimbutas, Noble.

p.119 • *Woman is raped.* US Department of Justice, *Crime in the United States, 1999.*

p.119 • *Bosnian women.* "Note to Correspondents," International Labour Organization, March 5, 2002.

p.119 • *Pregnant women are battered.* "Domestic Violence," American Prosecutors Research Institute.

p.119 • *Murder...leading cause of death.* I L Horon et.al., "Enhanced Surveillance for Pregnancy-Associated Mortality," *JAMA*, vol. 285, no. 11, March 21, 2001.

p.119 • *Hysterectomy...second most common major surgery.* "Fact sheet: Hysterectomy in the United States, 1980-1993," Centers for Disease Control.

p.119 • *Hysterectomies performed...unnecessary.* M S Broder et.al., "The appropriateness of recommendations for hysterectomy," *Obstetrics & Gynecology*, vol. 95, no. 2, February 2000, pp.199-205.

p.119 • *One-fourth of all American women...hysterectomy.* Centers for Disease Control, op.cit.

p.120 • *Caesarean...most common major surgery.* Agency for Healthcare Research and Quality, May 2000.

p.120 • *At least 22%.* L Neergaard, "Caesareans on the Rise," Associated Press, August 29, 2000.

p.120 • *Inquisition...eliminated common knowledge.* John Riddle, *Eve's Herbs: A History of Contraception and Abortion in the West.* Cambridge: Harvard University Press, 1997.

p.120 • *Educating women...illegal.* Rachel Galvin, "Margaret Sanger's 'Deeds of Terrible Virtue,'" *Newsletter*, National Endowment for the Humanities, September 1998; Janet Brodie, *Contraception and Abortion in 19th-Century America.* Ithaca: Cornell University Press, 1994.

p.121 • *Nearly half of all pregnancies...accidental.* "Talking About Freedom of Choice," NARAL Pro-Choice America Foundation, March 26, 2002.

p.121 • *5,000 women died annually.* "The Safety of Legal Abortion and the Hazards of Illegal Abortion," NARAL Pro-Choice America Foundation, January 20, 2003.

p.121 • *Reproductive technology.* Corea.

p.121 • *Law...requires a woman.* Robert Wayne Pelton, *Loony Laws That You Never Knew You Were Breaking.* New York: Walker, 1990, p. 34.

p.121 • *Corsets...social control.* Valerie Steele, *The Corset: A Cultural History.* New Haven: Yale University Press, 2001. Compressing her abdomen, a woman's corset could cause gastro-esophageal reflux disease (GERD). For at least one woman, the related scarring of her lung tissue led to repeated episodes— and a fatal case—of aspiration pneumonia. Personal communication, Sara Kingdon, MD, November 1998.

p.122 • *Tummy tucks.* The American Society for Aesthetic Plastic Surgery, *Cosmetic Surgery National Data Bank, 2002 Statistics.* 2002.

p.122 • *Self-mutilation.* Lindsay Utz, "Focusing on *Girl Culture*," *Arizona Daily Wildcat.* October 3, 2002.

p.122 • *80%...started dieting.* L M Mellin et.al., "Disordered eating characteristics in preadolescent girls," Meeting of the American Dietetic Association, 1986.

p.122 • *Dieting drastically increases...chance.* "Facts About Eating Disorders," National Association of Anorexia Nervosa and Associated Disorders.

p.122 • *Women in midlife.* G Bellafante, "When Midlife Seems Just an Empty Plate," *NY Times*, March 9, 2003.

p.122 • *Anorexia...leading cause of death.* John Barnhill et.al., *If You Think You Have an Eating Disorder.* New York: Dell, 1998.

p.123 • *Barbie.* "Among Barbie's first garments were two strapless brassieres, one half-slip, one floral petticoat, and—God knows why—a girdle." M G Lord, *Forever Barbie.* New York: William Morrow, 1994, p.34.

p.124 • *Pandora's box.* Walker, pp.160-161.

For information about eating disorders and related concerns, see links to service organizations listed at

www.loveyourbelly.com

• • •

References

Baring, Anne and Jules Cashford. *The Myth of the Goddess*. London: Viking, 1991.

Brennan, Barbara Ann. *Light Emerging: The journey of personal healing*. New York: Bantam, 1993.

Chang, Stephen. *The Crane Exercise: How to rub your stomach away*. 1985.

Claremont de Castillejo, Irene, *Knowing Woman: A feminine psychology*. Boston: Shambhala, 1997.

Chernin, Kim. *The Obsession: Reflections on the tyranny of slenderness*. San Francisco: HarperRow, 1981.

Cohen, Kenneth S. *The Way of Qigong: The art and science of Chinese energy healing*. New York: Ballantine Books, 1997.

Corea, Gena. *The Mother Machine: Reproductive technologies from artificial insemination to artificial wombs*. New York: Harper and Row, 1985.

Daly, Mary. *Beyond God the Father: Toward a philosophy of women's liberation*. Boston: Beacon Press, 1973.

Dürckheim, Karlfried Graf Von. *Hara: The Vital Centre of Man*. London: Unwin, 1962, 1977, 1984.

Eisler, Riane. *The Chalice and the Blade: Our history, our future*. San Francisco: Harper and Row, 1987.

Ellis, Andrew et.al. *Grasping the Wind*. Brookline, MA: Paradigm Publications, 1989.

Estés, Clarissa Pinkola. *Women Who Run With the Wolves: Myths and stories of the Wild Woman archetype*. New York: Ballantine, 1992.

Gadon, Elinor. *The Once and Future Goddess: A symbol for our time*. San Francisco: HarperRow, 1989.

Genelli, Lyn Davis. "Hanging Up Your Fat Suit." *Yoga Journal*. July/August 1989.

Gimbutas, Marija. *The Language of the Goddess: Unearthing the hidden symbols of Western civilization*. San Francisco: Harper and Row, 1989.

Hall, Nor. *The Moon and the Virgin: Reflections on the Archetypal Feminine*. New York: HarperCollins, 1980.

Hilber, Alison. *Change How You See, Not How You Look*. New Bern: Trafford, 2002.

Hollander, Anne. *Seeing Through Clothes*. New York: The Viking Press, 1978.

Judith, Anodea and Selene Vega. *The Sevenfold Journey: Reclaiming mind, body and spirit through the chakra*s. Freedom, CA: The Crossing Press, 1993.

• • •

References

Kelly, Mary. B. *Goddess Embroideries of Eastern Europe*. Winona, MN: Northland Press, 1989.

King, Serge. *The Aloha Spirit*. Kilauea, HI: Aloha International, 1990.

Lawlor, Robert. *Sacred Geometry: Philosophy and Practice*. London: Thames and Hudson, 1982.

Lubell, Winifred. *The Metamorphosis of Baubo: Myths of women's sexual energy*. Nashville: Vanderbilt University Press, 1994.

Masunaga, Shizuto. trans. Stephen Brown. *Meridian Exercises*. New York: Japan Publications, 1987.

Matsumoto, Kiiko and Stephen Birch. *Hara Diagnosis: Reflections on the Sea*. Brookline, MA: Paradigm Publications, 1988.

Noble, Vicki. *Shakti Woman: Feeling our fire, healing our world—the new female shamanism*. San Francisco: Harper and Row, 1991.

Oki, Masahiro. *Zen Yoga Therapy*. New York: Japan Publications, 1979.

Progoff, Ira. *At a Journal Workshop*. New York: Dialogue House, 1975.

Rainer, Tristine. *The New Diary*. Los Angeles: J P Tarcher, 1978.

Richards, M C. *Centering: In pottery, poetry, and the person*. Middletown, CT: Wesleyan University Press, 1964.

Ruiz, Fernando Pagés. "Forget Six-Pack Abs: Healthy abdominal muscles are strong, not hard." *Yoga Journal*. March/April 2001.

Starbird, Margaret. *The Woman with the Alabaster Jar: Mary Magdalen and the Holy Grail*. Santa Fe: Bear and Co, 1993.

Steele, Valerie. *Fashion and Eroticism: Ideals of feminine beauty from the Victorian era to the Jazz Age*. New York: Oxford University Press, 1985.

Walker, Barbara. *The Woman's Dictionary of Symbols and Sacred Objects*. San Francisco: Harper and Row, 1988.

Waters, Frank. *Book of the Hopi*. New York: Penguin Books, 1963.

Yamaoka, Seigen. *The Art and the Way of Hara*. rev. ed. Union City, CA: Heian International, 1992.

• • •

Resources

***Honoring Your Belly* seminars:** One-day workshops and weekend retreats provide a safe, welcoming, and playful environment for discovering your body's center as the site of your soul-power. The experience includes learning the full sequence of twenty-three belly-energizing exercises and engaging in dialogue, reflection, creative imagination, and laughter.

***Honoring Your Belly* instructional videotape:** This thirty-five minute video presents a circle of women moving through the full sequence of belly-energizing exercises as a twelve-minute practice. Then it presents instruction for each of the exercises individually. Once you're familiar with the moves, you're ready to join the circle and enjoy the support of a group practice.

Belly-celebrating accessories: A journal for recording your experience and insights plus t-shirts, tote bags, and more. See *Crafts for the Spirit* (Lark Books, 2003) for instructions for making your own decorative Belly Belt.

Teacher training: A professional program preparing you to teach *Honoring Your Belly* as a complement to your work as a counselor, yoga teacher, dance or movement arts instructor, or bodywork therapist.

Keynote speaking: Interactive presentations relating the value of woman's belly to any aspect of women's health, history, culture, and current events.

Continuing projects: A traveling art show featuring images that celebrate woman's belly. A video compiling belly-proud performance pieces. A collection of interviews with women and girls about how we're developing positive attitudes with respect to our bellies. Share your story—how you've changed the way you value and experience your body's center!

Blessed be!

Lisa Sarasohn
Self-Health Education
PO Box 1783
Asheville, NC 28802-1783
www.loveyourbelly.com
lisa@loveyourbelly.com

• • •

More praise for
The Woman's Belly Book

"*The Woman's Belly Book* is a hymn to the glory, grit and gorgeousness of the female gut. Every woman should read this book. When we can, without shame or guilt, reclaim the sacred power inherent in our woman-middles, the world will be a healthier, stronger and better place. And women will be healthier for loving our bodies."
—BYRON BALLARD, author of *Embracing Willendorf*

"*The Woman's Belly Book* stimulated a powerful spiritual awakening. Exploring the practical methods for releasing self-hating conditioning, I became more aware of the spiritual energy available to me. I learned to relax and enjoy my body, rather than feeling restricted by it. Viewing my body and my sexuality as sacred greatly enhanced my visceral connection with the source of universal love. Lisa's exercises and words are powerful medicine, graceful and inspiring."
—ELIZABETH FISHER, author of *Rise Up and Call Her Name: A woman-honoring journey into global earth-based spiritualities*

"This book is different from the hundreds, perhaps thousands, of books written on 'how to love yourself.' Not just because Lisa understands where body hatred comes from; not just because the book is filled with practical methodology and sage advice; not just because it is sprinkled with nuggets of profound wisdom. This book is different because you will come to understand that our survival as a species depends on women's bellies. So gather the women you know. Meet over it. Talk about it. Explore it. Laugh with it. Remind yourself of the time when women and our bellies were sacred."
—DEB LEMIRE, review in *Goddessing*

"This is a how-to book for putting into practice the decision to love ourselves in our bodies. Lisa's words are grounded in deep study of physiology, psychology, gender issues, cross-cultural spirituality, mythology and exercise, but her book is not theoretical. It offers a menu of simple gifts to enrich our appreciation for and connection with our bellies, the seat of our passion and the hope of the world. Ranging from breathing exercises to art projects, visualizations, life inventories, laughter coaching and writing prompts, the activities add up to a multi-media return to worship of the manifest source of life."
—DONNA GLEE WILLIAMS, PhD, review in *The Beltane Papers*

"*The Woman's Belly Book* is a blazing trail home to a woman's power, self-esteem, creativity, sexual energy, self-love, and respect for one's own beauty. Brilliantly, Lisa opens the veil to women's mysteries, to a place that every woman possesses but hardly dares to venture. Lisa will show you how to honor yourself here and be gentle with what surfaces. *The Woman's Belly Book* is a treasure map to finding and honoring the wisdom deep in you. Let's go mining for truth down there! Are you ready?"

—ALISA STARKWEATHER, founder, *Women's Belly & Womb Conference*